WHAT EVERY PRINCIPAL SHOULD KNOW ABOUT

INSTRUCTIONAL LEADERSHIP

JEFFREY GLANZ

CORWIN PRESS
A SAGE Publications Company
Thousand Oaks, California

For information:

Corwin Press
A Sage Publications Company
2455 Teller Road
Thousand Oaks, California 91320
E-mail: order@corwinpress.com

Sage Publications Ltd.
1 Oliver's Yard
55 City Road
London EC1Y 1SP
United Kingdom

Sage Publications India Pvt. Ltd.
B-42, Panchsheel Enclave
Post Box 4109
New Delhi 110 017 India

Printed in the United States of America.

Library of Congress Cataloging-in-Publication Data

Glanz, Jeffrey.
What every principal should know about instructional leadership / Jeffrey Glanz.
 p. cm.
Includes bibliographical references and index.
ISBN 978-1-4129-1586-1 (pbk.)
 1. School supervision. 2. School principals. 3. Teacher-principal
relationships. 4. Curriculum planning. I. Title.
LB2806.4.G5324 2006
 371.2'03—dc22   2005005354

This book is printed on acid-free paper.

07   08   09   10   9   8   7   6   5   4   3   2

Acquisitions Editor:	Elizabeth Brenkus
Editorial Assistant:	Candice L. Ling
Production Editor:	Tracy Alpern
Copy Editor:	Rachel Hile Bassett
Proofreader:	Christine Dahlin
Typesetter:	C&M Digitals (P) Ltd.
Indexer:	Gloria Tierney
Cover Designer:	Rose Storey

WHAT EVERY PRINCIPAL SHOULD KNOW ABOUT

INSTRUCTIONAL LEADERSHIP

WHAT EVERY PRINCIPAL SHOULD KNOW ABOUT LEADERSHIP
The 7-Book Collection

By Jeffrey Glanz

What Every Principal Should Know About Instructional Leadership

What Every Principal Should Know About Cultural Leadership

What Every Principal Should Know About Ethical and Spiritual Leadership

What Every Principal Should Know About School-Community Leadership

What Every Principal Should Know About Collaborative Leadership

What Every Principal Should Know About Operational Leadership

What Every Principal Should Know About Strategic Leadership

Contents

*To Mrs. Duncan, Mr. Schindler, Mr. Levitan,
Mr. Evans, Ms. Adams . . . each of whom served as a principal
with conviction and insight, and from whom I learned much
(including instructional leadership) while watching in the wings.*

Acknowledgments

Carl Glickman once astutely commented, "The reason everyone goes into education is to have a powerful influence on the educational lives of students." Those uniquely talented who aspire to the principalship sincerely want to make a difference. They realize that they are in an optimal position to effect great change and provide for the larger "good." They are driven by an unyielding commitment to facilitate the conditions necessary to foster high achievement for all students. As managers, advocates, planners, mentors, supervisors, and above all else leaders, they establish a conducive tone in a school building that serves to promote educational excellence at all levels. Not far removed from the classroom, principals realize that in order for students to excel academically, an instructional program must be established that is rigorous, sustained, and meaningful. As instructional leaders, they are the most critical element in promoting exceptional teaching that aims to improve student learning. This book and series are dedicated to all who aspire to the principalship, currently serve as principals, or who have been principals. No nobler an enterprise and profession exists, for principals are the "teachers of teachers."

* * * * * * * * * * * * * * *

Thanks to my acquisitions editor, Lizzie Brenkus, for her gentle encouragement and support. She always responded to my flurry of e-mails and calls promptly and with grace. Many thanks go to Robb Clouse, editorial director, who prompted me to consider a trilogy of sorts: a book about teaching, which eventuated into *Teaching 101*; a book about assistant principals, which led to *The Assistant Principal's Handbook*; and a book about principals, which resulted to my surprise in this groundbreaking series, *What Every Principal Should Know About Leadership.*

Special thanks to my wife, Lisa, without whose support such a venture would be impossible. I love you . . . at least as much as I love writing.

Corwin Press gratefully acknowledges the contributions of the following individuals:

Regina Birdsell, Principal
Academy School
Madison, CT

Dana Trevethan, Principal
Turlock High School
Turlock, CA

Judy Carr, Associate
    Professor
College of Education
University of South Florida
Sarasota, FL

Paul Young, Principal,
    Author
West Elementary School
Lancaster, OH

James Halley, Superintendent
    of Schools
North Kingstown School
    District
North Kingstown, RI

About the Author

 **Jeffrey Glanz**, **EdD**, currently serves as Dean of Graduate Programs and Chair of the Department of Education at Wagner College in Staten Island, New York. He also coordinates the educational leadership program that leads to New York State certification as a principal or assistant principal. Prior to arriving at Wagner, he served as executive assistant to the president of Kean University in Union, New Jersey. Dr. Glanz held faculty status as a tenured professor in the Department of Instruction and Educational Leadership at Kean University's College of Education. He was named Graduate Teacher of the Year in 1999 by the Student Graduate Association and was also that year's recipient of the Presidential Award for Outstanding Scholarship. He served as an administrator and teacher in the New York City public schools for 20 years. Dr. Glanz has authored, coauthored, or coedited 13 books and has more than 35 peer-reviewed article publications. With Corwin Press he coauthored the best selling *Supervision That Improves Teaching* (2nd ed.) and *Supervision in Practice: Three Steps to Improve Teaching and Learning* and authored *The Assistant Principal's Handbook* and *Teaching 101: Classroom Strategies for the Beginning Teacher.* More recently he coauthored *Building Effective Learning Communities: Strategies for Leadership, Learning, & Collaboration.* Most recently, Dr. Glanz has authored the *What Every Principal Should Know About Leadership: The 7-Book Collection:*

> *What Every Principal Should Know About Instructional Leadership*
>
> *What Every Principal Should Know About Cultural Leadership*

Consult his Web site for additional information: http://www
.wagner.edu/faculty/users/jglanz/web/

* * * * * * * * * * * * * * *

The "About the Author" information you've just glanced at (excuse the pun . . . my name? . . . Glanz, "glance"?!) is standard author bio info you find in most books. As you'll discover if you glance at . . . I mean *read* . . . the Introduction, I want this book to be user-friendly in several ways. One of the ways is that I want to write as I would converse with you in person. Therefore, I prefer in most places to use the first person, so please excuse the informality. Although we've likely never met, we really do know each other if you think about it. We share a common passion about leadership, school building leadership to be more precise. We share many similar experiences. In an experiential, almost spiritual, sense, we have much in common. What I write about directly relates, I hope, to your lived experience. The information in this volume, as with the entire series, is meant to resonate, stir, provoke, and provide ideas about principal leadership, which is vital in order to promote excellence and achievement for all.

This traditional section of a book is titled "About the Author." The first paragraph in this section tells you what I "do," not "about" me or who I am. I won't bore you with all details "about me," but I'd like just to share one bit of info that communicates more meaningfully about "me" than the information in the first paragraph. I am (I presume like you) passionate about what I do. I love to teach, guide, mentor, learn, supervise, and lead. For me, leadership is self-preservation. Personally and professionally, I strive to do my very best, to use whatever God-given leadership talents I possess to make a difference in the lives of others. I continually strive to improve myself intellectually and socially, but also physically and spiritually. Family and community are very important to me. Building and sustaining community is integral to my professional practice. I see myself as part of a larger community of learners as we share, experience, overcome difficulties, learn from our mistakes, and in the end help others (students, colleagues, and community members) achieve their educational goals.

If any of the information in this book series touches you in any way, please feel free to contact me by using my personal e-mail address: tora.dojo@verizon.net. I encourage you to share your reactions, comments, and suggestions or simply to relate an anecdote or two, humorous or otherwise, that may serve as "information from the field" for future editions of this work, ultimately to help others. Your input is much appreciated.

Questionnaire: Before We Get Started . . .

Directions: Using the Likert scale below, circle the answer that best represents your on-the-spot belief about each statement. The questionnaire serves as an advanced organizer of sorts for some of the key topics in this book, although items are purposely constructed in no particular order. Discussion of each topic, though, occurs within the context of relevant chapters. Responses or views to each statement are presented in a subsection following the questionnaire (this section begins "Now, let's analyze your responses . . ."). You may or may not agree with the points made, but I hope you will be encouraged to reflect on your own views. Reflective activities follow to allow for deeper analysis. Elaboration of ideas emanating from this brief activity will occur throughout the text and series. I encourage you to share reflections (yours and mine) with colleagues. I'd appreciate your personal feedback via the e-mail address I've listed in the "About the Author" section.

SA = Strongly Agree ("For the most part, yes.")

A = Agree ("Yes, but . . .")

D = Disagree ("No, but . . .")

SD = Strongly Disagree ("For the most part, no.")

SA   A   D   SD   1. To be effective, the principal must have
                          been a successful classroom teacher.

SA   A   D   SD   2. Good principals must know how to facilitate best practices in teaching, curriculum, and supervision.

SA   A   D   SD   3. It is reasonable to expect a principal to serve as a presenter in a professional development session.

SA   A   D   SD   4. It is reasonable to expect principals to know as much or more about wait time, Bloom's Taxonomy, and differentiated instruction than teachers.

SA   A   D   SD   5. It is reasonable to expect principals to lead disciplinary instruction in mathematics, biology, English, history, and so forth.

SA   A   D   SD   6. The principal should spend many hours on the job in the classroom each day.

SA   A   D   SD   7. The principal should be the most important instructional leader in a school.

SA   A   D   SD   8. The principal is the single greatest factor in determining the extent of student achievement.

SA   A   D   SD   9. Instructional leadership should take priority over other forms of leadership.

SA   A   D   SD   10. I am comfortable facilitating instructional leadership in my school.

Before we analyze your responses, consider that our beliefs about what we do greatly influence our actions. Although we realize that what we profess and say we believe—our "espoused theories"—are not always congruent with what we do—our "theory-in-use"—articulating beliefs is important (Osterman & Kottkamp, 2004). For example, if you believe that a principal need not have been a successful teacher, then you will likely maintain that instructional improvement, although certainly important, can be facilitated by or delegated to others. In other words, you might say, "I don't have to have been a teacher in order to understand the importance of teaching and learning, and in order to facilitate an instructional program."

I believe that such an assertion is not only wrongheaded, but potentially detrimental to the education of boys and girls in schools. I believe that the principal serves as the foremost instructional leader in the school building. Your commitment to instructional improvement must not only be strongly articulated but must also be reinforced with experience in the classroom. I don't think that you had to be the "teacher of the year," but I believe that at least 3 to 5 years of successful teaching experience is imperative, not only to gain legitimacy in the eyes of teachers (i.e., you have "walked the talk") but also so that you understand the instructional challenges faced by teachers with firsthand experience.

I believe that operational managerial, strategic, collaborative, and cultural leadership abilities are certainly important but that prior experiences with fostering such leadership, although an asset, should not necessarily be the sole precondition for assuming the principalship. Instructional leadership, however, demands, in my view, that you are committed to high standards of academic excellence, set high expectations for student success, and have had some firsthand experience with effective teaching or instructional strategies. Now, I don't mean to say that all good teachers would make successful principals. Not all good teachers are fit for the principalship. Other forms of leadership qualities, dispositions, and competencies are certainly necessary. What I am saying is that the principal must have a good experiential sense of the instructional process in order to effectively facilitate best teaching practices that promote high achievement for all students.

The principal is not the sole instructional leader. Rather, a good principal identifies a community of instructional leaders who collaborate as a learning community to examine teaching practices that best promote student learning. Principals, therefore, at their best facilitate good instructional practice. To do so, however, requires experience as a teacher in some context at some time. When it comes to promoting instructional excellence, there's nothing like experience.

These ideas are fundamental. Consider the following reflective questions as you consider the meaning of instructional leadership:

Reflective Questions

1. Which of the belief statements above resonates the most with you?

2. Which of the views expressed above do you disagree with? Explain.

3. If you believe that a principal need not have been a teacher, how can the principal gain instructional legitimacy with teachers, and more important, what must she or he do to positively influence student achievement?

4. Recall principals you have known, and consider the degree to which they had experience in the classroom. Which principals served as good instructional leaders, and did their experience in the classroom help or hinder their role? Conversely, consider principals who have little, if any, classroom experience, and explain how successful they have been as instructional leaders. What other factors are important in order to promote instructional leadership?

---

* * * * * * * * * * * * * * *

Examine these quotations on the importance of an instructional leader. What do they mean to you?

"A school learning community must hold curriculum, instruction, and assessment central to its work if it expects to make a difference for student learning. The principal's role has evolved from manager to instructional leader to facilitator-leader of the school learning community. Through collaborative work of the principal and teachers, curriculum development and instructional and assessment practices continually change to conform to the needs of all students. Curriculum, instruction, and assessment are the heart of the school learning community. The role of the principal is to facilitate and keep the school focused on excellent curriculum, instruction, and assessment to meet students' learning needs and improve achievement."

—Marsha Speck

"The key factor to the individual school's success is the building principal, who sets the tone as the school's educational leader."

—Arthur Anderson

"The principals of tomorrow's schools must be instructional leaders who possess the requisite skills, capacities, and commitment to lead the accountability parade, not follow it. Excellence in school leadership should be recognized as the most important component of school reform. Without leadership, the chances for systemic improvement in teaching and learning are nil."

—Gerald N. Tirozzi

"Good principals make good teaching and learning possible."

—Robert D. Ramsey

"The most important person in the school is the principal."

—Hillary Rodham Clinton

"Never underestimate the importance of instructional leadership. . . . Effective principals do not allow managerial tasks to consume their days. They create adequate time to focus on being the instructional leaders of their schools. It is the key part of their job."

—Paul G. Young

* * * * * * * * * * * * * * * *

Now, let's analyze your responses to the questionnaire:

1. To be effective, the principal must have been a successful classroom teacher.
   Successful, yes, not necessarily the best.

2. Good principals must know how to facilitate best practices in teaching, curriculum, and supervision.
   Yes, and facilitate *is the key word.*

3. It is reasonable to expect a principal to serve as a presenter in a professional development session.
   Yes. Not the sole presenter, but a principal should feel comfortable enough to "show the way" by demonstrating sound teaching practices, to communicate to others "do as I do, not just as I say."

4. It is reasonable to expect principals to know as much or more about wait time, Bloom's Taxonomy, and differentiated instruction than teachers.
   No. Although principals are somewhat conversant with ideas in each area, they are not experts and should therefore reach out to others; the principal serves here as a discussant of these areas with teachers.

5. It is reasonable to expect principals to lead disciplinary instruction in mathematics, biology, English, history, and so forth.
   No. The words of Wilmore (2004) are instructive here:

Yet even though you are the instructional leader, there is nothing that requires you to be the expert in all forms of language, mathematics, science, technology, history, and civic responsibility. What you are required to do is to understand and facilitate appropriate processes for curriculum enhancement and developmentally appropriate instructional methods. . . . You are the facilitator of these areas, not the sole provider of them. (p. 51)

6. The principal should spend many hours on the job in the classroom each day.

Not necessarily. Although a principal who believes in and feels comfortable dealing with instructional matters spends a large part of the day thinking about and facilitating instruction, it is equally unreasonable that the principal needs to spend literally hours in the classroom. However, you will notice that principals who have not been successful teachers and are uncomfortable or not knowledgeable about teaching, for instance, will avoid the classroom or spend just a few moments "shooting the breeze" with teachers and students in the classroom.

7. The principal should be the most important instructional leader in a school.

Yes, but not the sole leader. Allow me to quote Wilmore (2004) once again:

Be careful to notice the difference between being able to facilitate the successful progress of teachers and others, rather than doing everything yourself. If you try to do that, you will kill yourself. Once dead, there isn't anything you can do to help anyone, so budget your time. (p. 51)

8. The principal is the single greatest factor in determining the extent of student achievement.

Yes and no. Promoting student achievement is a complex process that involves many school/classroom/community contextual variables. Although the teacher is certainly the key individual in the classroom, influencing student learning on a daily basis, the principal can be viewed as an orchestra leader of sorts who coordinates, facilitates, and oversees the instructional process on a schoolwide basis. The principal as orchestra leader, seen in this way, is the most important link or ingredient to ensure high student achievement.

9. Instructional leadership should take priority over other forms of leadership.

All forms of leadership (see other titles in this book series) work synchronously, that is, in unison with one another. Although it is diffi-cult to separate instructional from cultural leadership as well as from other forms of leadership, the principal, I assert, should be primarily focused in a strategic way on promoting high instructional standards that encourage exceptional teaching and that yield high achievement for all students.

10. I am comfortable facilitating instructional leadership in my school.

This is a statement each of you must assess on your own. If you have not had successful or sufficient experience in the classroom, all is not lost. You must engage in strong and ongoing personal professional development in this area. The more you read, the more workshops you attend, and the more you practice your instructional skills, the more legitimacy you'll have in the eyes of teachers and the more likely you'll positively influence the school's instructional program.

Reflective Questions

1. Which of the explanations above makes the most sense to you?

2. Which of the explanations above makes the least sense to you? Explain why.

3. What additional information might you need to know before making a decision or taking a viewpoint either way?

See Resource B for a more detailed survey to assess your role as instructional leader.

C H A P T E R   O N E

Introduction

"Effective school leadership, in the form of a dedicated, skilled principal, is a key element in creating and maintaining high quality schools."

—Philip A. Cusick

Practice since the early 20th century, when the principalship assumed a prominent role in schools (Beck & Murphy, 1993), and research ever since the School Effectiveness Studies in the 1980s (DeRoche, 1987) affirm the vital role of the principal in terms of establishing an effective and efficient school. With the advent of the federal "No Child Left Behind" Act of 2001, the principal has been viewed, perhaps more than ever before, not only as essential for creating and sustaining a well-run school, but most important, as critical for promoting student achievement (Matthew & Crow, 2003).

As recently as 15 years ago, principals were largely responsible only for ensuring a safe school building, managing bus schedules, keeping order by enforcing district and school policies, developing master schedules, ordering books and supplies, and other logistical managerial tasks. According to Paul Young (2004), "That principalship doesn't exist anymore" (p. 50). Though still accountable for these and other managerial tasks, principals today are ultimately responsible for providing top-quality instructional leadership that aims to promote best practices in teaching and related instructional areas for the chief purpose of ensuring student achievement. Overseeing and delegating responsibilities to ensure a safe and secure school building are important, but good principals today focus on instruction, because they know that doing so, more than *anything else they do*, directly affects student learning. According to Young (2004), good principals

> must be viewed as guides and coaches, leaders who establish high expectations and common direction . . . [they] regularly observe classrooms, guide lesson planning, create common planning time, monitor student learning, collect data, and use results to influence improvement plans. (p. 51)

Although important as ever, the principal today faces more demands, more complex decisions, and more responsibilities than principals of the past. The knowledge, skills, and dispositions needed to become a successful principal of yesteryear are no longer adequate today. This book series is meant to provide you with the theory and tools necessary to meet the challenges, demands, and crises facing schools in the 21st century (Schlechty, 1990).

Principals are busy people; they are also consummate professionals. Many books serve as texts in graduate courses leading to a master's degree or state certification as a school administrator or principal. These books contain a great deal of important information—sometimes too much to be absorbed in just a short period of time. Much of the information they contain, albeit important, is often forgotten or overlooked, because the information really comes into play when people are on the job. No wonder so many principals indicate that much of what they learned in principal preparation courses in graduate school isn't relevant. It's not that these programs aren't sound; they do provide essential information. It's just the nature of the way theory and practices are bifurcated. This book, then, culls, in a concise, easy-to-read manner, only essential knowledge, skills, and dispositions needed to get started in the principalship. It certainly doesn't represent all you ever need to know. No book or even series can do that. The principalship, like teaching or any educational enterprise, is a lifelong learning process.

The major themes or underlying assumptions of this book and series on the principalship are the following:

- The principal is *the* key player in the school building to promote student learning. It's not that students can't learn without a principal, of course; teachers play no small role in the classroom. But a specially trained instructional leader serving as building principal is vital in order to accomplish deep, sustained, and schoolwide achievement for all students.

- High achievement for all students is the major goal for a principal. A principal may possess charisma, increase parental participation in school activities, raise funds for the PTA, organize meaningful cultural events, or even possess great vision. However, the bottom line is that a principal first and foremost is concerned in activities that actively promote good teaching, which in turn promotes student learning. A principal cannot be considered successful unless high student achievement in academic areas is achieved.

- The principal must play an active, ongoing role in instructional leadership. The comprehensive study *Making Sense of Leading Schools: A Study of the School Principalship* (Portin, 2003) indicated that principals do not necessarily have to have expertise in all areas (e.g., instructional, cultural, managerial, human resources, strategic, external development, micropolitical leadership), but they must be master "diagnosticians," able to provide the school what it needs at the right time and in the right context. Nevertheless, I maintain that instructional leadership is qualitatively different from other forms of leadership. Although it's difficult to separate each form of leadership from another, because they all form an undifferentiated whole, instructional leadership can never be simply delegated to others. Others serve as instructional leaders for sure, but the principal plays an active and orchestrating role.

- Simply stated, leadership matters. Research has continually demonstrated that leadership is critical for school success (Portin, 2004). More recently, data indicate that a substantial relationship exists between leadership and student achievement. According to Waters, Marzano, and McNulty (2004), who report on a 25-year-old continuing study on leadership by the Mid-continent

Research for Education and Learning (McREL) group, there is a significant, positive correlation between effective school leadership and student achievement. An effect size of .25 between leadership and student achievement indicates that as leadership improves, so does student achievement. The report also indicated that instructional leadership matters most. Although effective leadership comprises many key areas of principal behavior (e.g., good communication, high visibility in the community, etc.), a principal's focus on instruction, curriculum, and assessment is most important in terms of promoting student achievement. This book, therefore, emphasizes the important and most necessary requirement—that a principal serve as an instructional leader—and in doing so, her or his leadership matters.

This book and series are also aligned with standards established by the prominent Educational Leadership Constituent Council (ELCC). ELCC standards are commonly accepted by most educational organizations concerned with preparing high-quality educational leaders and as such are most authoritative (Wilmore, 2002). The ELCC, an arm of the National Council for the Accreditation of Teacher Education, developed six leadership standards used widely in principal preparation. These standards formed the basis for this book and series:

1.0: Candidates who complete the program are educational leaders who have the knowledge and ability to promote the success of all students by facilitating the development, articulation, implementation, and stewardship of a school or district vision of learning supported by the school community.

*2.0: Candidates who complete the program are educational leaders who have the knowledge and ability to promote the success of all students by promoting a positive school culture, providing an effective instructional program, applying best practices to student learning, and designing comprehensive professional growth plans for staff.

3.0: Candidates who complete the program are educational leaders who have the knowledge and ability to promote the success of all students by managing the organization, operations, and resources in a way that promotes a safe, efficient, and effective learning environment.

4.0: Candidates who complete the program are educational leaders who have the knowledge and ability to promote the success of all students by collaborating with families and other community members, responding to diverse community interests and needs, and mobilizing community resources.

5.0: Candidates who complete the program are educational leaders who have the knowledge and ability to promote the success of all students by acting with integrity, fairly, and in an ethical manner.

6.0: Candidates who complete the program are educational leaders who have the knowledge and ability to promote the success of all students by understanding, responding to, and influencing the larger political, social, economic, legal, and cultural context.

* This standard is addressed in the present book.

Readers should also familiarize themselves with the Interstate School Leaders Licensure Consortium and National Association of Elementary School Principals standards (see, e.g., http://www.ccsso.org/projects/Interstate_School_Leaders_Licensure_Consortium/ and http://www.boyercenter.org/basicschool/naesp.shtml). Another important point to make in this introduction is that some administrators claim they have little time to devote to instructional leadership. In fact, many claim they have scant time for anything educational. According to J. Johnson (2004), "Nearly three in four principals say that daily emergencies eat into time that they would rather spend on education issues" (p. 24). Certainly, we acknowledge the increased expectations and challenges placed on principals by local, state, and federal reform initiatives, along with the exigencies they face in running a school on a daily basis. However, exemplary principals find the time for what's really important. Skills of organization, delegation, and coordination are critical in order to devote time to what really matters. If principals really feel comfortable and committed to instruction, they will find the time.

Reflective Questions

1. Which of the themes or assumptions above make the most sense to you?

2. Which of the themes or assumptions above make the least sense to you? Explain.

3. How do you find or how do you intend to find the time for instructional leadership? Be specific.

---

* * * * * * * * * * * * * * * *

Allow me to offer a word on chapter format and presentation of information. Information in each of the three main chapters is presented as concisely as possible to make for easy and quick reference reading. Each chapter begins with boxed material called "What You Should Know About." The box will list and briefly explain the concepts covered in each chapter. In most cases, a principal (or his or her representative) can conduct a workshop for teachers on most of the topics listed. Certainly, each chapter will not cover every bit of information there is to know about a given topic, as mentioned earlier. Each chapter culls, though, essential knowledge, skills, and dispositions necessary for a successful principal.

The following box serves as a summary of this introduction by highlighting three research-based ideas about instructional leadership that should serve as checkpoints for your own progress as an instructional leader:

Three Research-Based Findings About the Activities of an Effective Instructional Leader

Committed to instructional leadership, good principals know, among other things, the following:

1. The single greatest influence on students in a classroom is the teacher. "Teachers have a powerful, long-lasting influence on their students" (Stronge, 2002, p. vii). Good principals support good teachers by providing instructional services and resources

on a continuing basis. Moreover, good principals attract and hire certified teachers who have specific knowledge, skills, and dispositions that are essential to promote student achievement; certified teachers are more successful than unlicensed teachers. Good principals also realize that retaining good teachers is essential because experience counts. "Experienced teachers differ from rookie teachers in that they have attained expertise through real-life experiences, classroom practice, and time" (Stronge, 2002, p. 9). Research demonstrates that teachers with more experience plan better, apply a range of teaching strategies, understand students' learning needs, and better organize instruction. Good principals understand this research.

2. An emphasis on academics is crucial. Effective principal instructional leaders spend much time discussing the instructional program with colleagues, teachers, parents, students, and district office leaders. They use every available opportunity to discuss instruction: personal informal and formal contacts with teachers, memoranda, e-mail communications, grade and faculty conferences, assembly programs, parent meetings, and so forth. They realize that establishing an orderly environment conducive to educational excellence is necessary. Good principals set high expectations and standards for success (Squires, Huitt, & Segars, 1984). In addition, and more specifically related to instructional improvement, effective principals:

- Establish clearly defined academic goals for the school (by grade)
- Collaboratively develop clear and consistent schoolwide instructional policies
- Examine instructional grouping patterns to ensure student mastery of content
- Ensure that instructional time is protected (more on time on task later in Chapter 1, but good principals make sure to minimize intrusions, e.g., excessive announcements over the loudspeaker, intrusive attendance report collection by office monitors, etc., all of which interrupt and compromise classroom teaching and learning)
- Monitor adherence to local or state standards in the curriculum
- Maintain a systematic method of assessment procedures
- Review data collected as a result of implementation of an assessment system

(Continued)

- Share and use the data to help improve the instructional school program
- Observe teachers and students engaged in the learning process
- Involve teachers in curriculum planning and decision making
- Assist teachers who are having instructional difficulties
- Provide for meaningful, ongoing, collaboratively developed professional development opportunities

3. The three primary elements of successful instructional leadership are as follows (Blase & Blase, 2004):

   a. Conducting instructional conferences is a primary element of successful instructional leadership. Whether involved in pre- or postobservation conferences, informal or more formal grade conferences, and so on, principals exhibit these behaviors: make suggestions, give feedback, model, use inquiry, and solicit opinions from teachers.

   b. Providing staff development is a second primary element of successful instructional leadership.

      Behaviors associated with providing staff development include emphasizing the study of teaching and learning, support for collaboration, development of coaching relationships, use of action research, provision of resources, and application of the principles of adult growth and development to all phases of the staff development program. (p. 162)

   c. Developing teacher reflection is a third primary element of successful instructional leadership. Principals purposefully engage teachers in articulating feelings, sharing attitudes, and thinking deeply about instructional issues.

CASE STUDY AND REFLECTIVE QUESTIONS

The alarm startled her as she squinted at the clock, revealing 4:02 a.m. Perfunctorily, she silenced the alarm, took a few deep breaths, and then suddenly popped out of bed. An avid biker and overall fitness enthusiast,

Melissa quickly donned her biking attire, grabbed some orange juice, and headed for the shed. For the next serene 40 minutes, she would speed through the picturesque bike path not far from her home overlooking the sea coast. For Melissa, the daily solitary journey energized her like no early-morning vitamin could. Hypnotically, she would take in the scenery as the breeze of the early morning cooled her face. She enjoyed spending some of this time reflecting on her day's activities. This quiet time for Melissa served two purposes. She benefited from some early-morning exercise, without which she couldn't function, and the solitude allowed her to strategize; she thought best while exercising in this manner.

In the office by 6:15 a.m. every morning, Melissa Tofigbakhsh, undisturbed aside from the usual small talk with Ray the custodian, sifts through myriad memoranda, policy statements, requisition forms, evaluation documents, and other paperwork. Dr. Tofigbakhsh is a self-starter, a highly energetic, strong-willed, and creative woman. The first in her family to attend college, teaching was her passion. "Melissa is a natural; students are attracted to her sincere demeanor and enthusiasm for her subject," explains Tom Healy, her first principal. Her second principal, Steve Isman, realized that she would not remain a teacher for very long, because "she was eager to find new and creative ways to make a difference in the lives of students." She had a reputation as an energetic, intelligent, and caring staff developer in her district. "Dr. Tofigbakhsh [was] as conversant with balanced literacy, differentiated instruction, and Socratic seminars as she was with technology as a teaching tool." Another one of her colleagues comments, "She was a much sought-after workshop leader; she was able to connect with her audience as she spoke to their lived experiences in the classroom."

After assuming the principalship in a neighboring district, Melissa put her talents to work. She actualized her passion for teaching and teachers by developing the district's prototype for sustained, collaborative, and practically relevant professional development seminars. Her commitment to instructional excellence, above all else, was obvious to all. Teachers appreciated her insights because she "walked the talk." "Dr. Tofigbakhsh is not at all condescending. She solicits your input, is a good listener, and knows her stuff," one teacher comments. Another reports, "It seems that we always are discussing what's happening in the classroom . . . I mean, instructionally. She cares, she listens, advises, and shows the way. She respects our own expertise, yet she offers insights and ideas that are helpful."

Melissa enjoys the early morning, because she prioritizes her time during the day and appreciates having a chance to deal with what she calls "administrivia of the previous day" before the school day officially begins. Her early-morning Instructional Council, from 7:45 to 8:35 a.m. two mornings a week, is open to everyone, including paraprofessionals, student teachers, parents, students, and of course teachers. Voluntary, the meeting time affords staff the opportunity to discuss any aspect of the instructional program, from workshop topics to sharing teaching strategies to arranging for guest speakers. "Dr. Tofigbakhsh is admired and respected," explains Beverley Harris, the district's deputy superintendent. "She places priority on what really matters, instruction."

Each morning, Melissa blocks out 2 hours on her calendar for various activities that include doing walk-throughs, conferring with teachers, conducting demo lessons, observing teachers and students interact, listening to teachers' instructional challenges, and offering some advice or suggestions when appropriate. Melissa finds this early-morning time most valuable in that "it's the quiet part of the day, and it allows me to focus on instruction. Besides, it's what I love to do." As the day wears on, emergencies arise, parents call, district office administrators request information, and student misbehavior issues must be dealt with. Although she divides responsibilities for attending to these noninstructional matters with her assistant principals, Melissa handles her fair share of them as well. Although she oversees lunchroom activities and daily scheduling and responds to never-ending e-mails and a host of other administrative matters in the school, she insists that principals "can find the time for attending to instructional leadership. It's a matter of not compromising what you believe is most important. Once you demonstrate your priorities, others (secretaries, custodians, district office officials, and teachers) will realize and respect your passion. It's even contagious."

In the late afternoon, she sets aside 45 minutes each day, barring an emergency, to meet with a teacher, offer a seminar at a grade conference, plan a professional development session, meet with a group of teachers, or deal with any instructional dilemma that might have arisen. "Ann, my secretary, knows not to disturb me. Although she feels at times she needs an answer to a particular problem, she knows this time for me is important. She understands, though, the difference between an 'important' matter and an 'urgent' one." She continues, "Teachers also realize that this time I spend is not meant to discuss a bake sale or any other noninstructional matter. It's time for anything instructionally related—from dealing with a recalcitrant student to developing more thought-provoking questions to cooperative learning strategies."

Melissa also realizes that building sustained professional development initiatives requires a team approach to instructional leadership. She identifies teachers and others in the school and district who volunteer to form an Instructional Leadership Team to plan and coordinate purposeful, participatory, knowledge-based, ongoing, developmental, analytic, and reflective professional development sessions.

"Educational excellence is the core of what I do as principal," *Melissa is fond of explaining. "Resource and facilities management, although necessary, merely provides the foundation and support in order to carry out our core mission, that of ensuring educational excellence through strong, uncompromising instructional leadership."*

Reflective Questions

1. Why do you think Dr. Tofigbakhsh is an effective instructional leader?

2. What strategies does Dr. Tofigbakhsh incorporate to provide for instructional leadership?

3. Would any of these strategies work for you? Explain why or why not. Be specific.

4. Do you agree with her approach to instructional leadership? Explain.

5. Explain what factors would preclude or permit your using her instructional leadership approach.

6. What other strategies could you suggest to make time for instructional leadership?

CHAPTER TWO

Best Practices in Teaching

"Before I stepped into my first classroom as a teacher, I thought teaching was mainly instruction, partly performing, certainly being in front and at the center of classroom life. Later, with much chaos and some pain, I learned that this is the least of it—teaching includes a more splendorous range of actions. Teaching is instructing, advising, counseling, organizing, assessing, guiding, goading, showing, managing, modeling, coaching, disciplining, prodding, preaching, persuading, proselytizing, listening, interacting, nursing, and inspiring."

—Gloria Ladson-Billings

Instructional leadership is about encouraging best practices in teaching. To do so requires principals to become familiar with innovative teaching theories and practices and to encourage teachers to model them in classrooms. Successful instructional leaders facilitate best practices in teaching in the following ways, among others:

- Model best practice in teaching as you, the principal, conduct workshops or even conduct meetings with and for teachers (e.g., use of wait time and thought-provoking questions: see rest of chapter).

- Allow fellow teachers to intervisit with each other so that they can see each other teach and generate and share teaching ideas among themselves.
- Visit other school sites in the district where best teaching practices are well known, and even encourage teachers to visit in order to bring back fresh ideas and different ways of doing things.
- Invite workshop leaders from within and outside of the school to conduct sessions on topics that teachers wish to learn about.

The following boxed material summarizes the teaching ideas highlighted in this chapter. The list is not exhaustive but is merely meant to highlight some key concepts and ideas that successful instructional leaders should know about as they conduct seminars and workshops and collaborate with teachers. Brief reflective activities follow each major concept to provoke thought on ways to implement ideas or to provide further understanding of each idea.

What You Should Know About Teaching

- **Reflective Practice**—is a process by which instructional leaders take the time to contemplate and assess the instructional needs of their schools, identify problem areas, and develop strategies for becoming more effective.
- **Preplanning**—occurs when teachers actively consider learning objectives and other preparatory lesson activities.
- **Allocated, Instructional, Engaged, and Success Time**—are crucial factors in promoting student learning.
- **Wait Time**—increases the amount of time students have to think before responding.
- **Direct Teaching**—refers to the time spent in actual teaching as opposed to nonteaching activities (e.g., collecting assignments).
- **Literacy Development** (including **Reciprocal Teaching**)—is essential regardless of what subject is taught.

(Continued)

- **Differentiated Instruction**—refers to the varied teaching strategies employed by teachers to address the learning needs of all students.
- **Divergent Questioning**—encourages deep and critical thinking.
- **Self-Assessment**—occurs when teachers begin to reflect or see themselves teaching.
- **Constructivism**—refers to learning by doing or active learning.

1. REFLECTIVE PRACTICE

"Reflection? Who has the time?" asks a principal in an inner-city school in Los Angeles. "Certainly, we've learned about 'reflective practice' in graduate courses, but who has much time to really 'reflect' when you're on the job?" complains a principal in a suburban school in Westchester, New York.

One of the most important decisions an instructional leader must make is whether or not to become a "reflective practitioner." A reflective leader is someone who takes the time to think about what has transpired or what steps should be taken tomorrow to improve the instructional program. A reflective leader thinks before acting. She or he is proactive, not reactive. A reflective leader takes responsibility for making those tough decisions and is willing to admit error. Reflective leaders do not act impulsively or overreact to a situation. Instead, they carefully consider options and decide on a course of action (Schon, 1987).

> *"The leadership we need is available in all of us. We have only to make it manifest."*
>
> —Harris Owen

Reflection is the heart of professional practice (Osterman & Kottkamp, 2004). Robert Starratt (1995) explains that

> practitioners who analyze the uniqueness of a problem confronting them, frame the problem in ways that structure its intelligibility, think about the results of their actions, and puzzle out why things worked and why they did not tend to build up a reservoir of insights and intuitions that they can call upon as they go about their work. (p. 66)

Overwhelmed and sometimes incapable of dealing with increased demands, educational leaders think that reflection-on-action is impossible when in fact, it is not only possible, but indeed essential (Whitaker, 1995). How then can an educational leader find the time to become a "reflective educator"? Here are some suggestions:

1. Set aside 15–30 minutes a day for reflective thinking. Build time into your schedule by informing your secretary that between 11:20 a.m. and 11:45 a.m., you are not to be disturbed, unless an emergency arises (and do give your secretary some examples of "legitimate" emergencies). During this time, you should close and lock your door and deliberate on the overall structure of the day or on one specific issue.

2. Some leaders prefer to "reflect" early in the morning before school begins or after school. Time for reflection should be determined by your schedule and preference. Choose a time when you are alert and can seriously contemplate the many issues that need attention. Personally, I'm a late-night person and find that 1:00 a.m. suits me just fine. I am most productive when the house is quiet and I'm able to think undisturbed.

3. One principal I had the opportunity to work with held a "cabinet meeting" every day from 7:30 a.m. until around 8:30 a.m., before students arrived. Such meetings allowed supervisory personnel to "reflect" and bring up important issues for general discussion. Anyone on the faculty or staff was allowed to attend these meetings to share their concerns or simply join in on "reflecting."

4. Delegate, delegate, and then delegate some more, but ensure accountability. You can't do it alone. Sustain school leadership by empowering others, especially your assistant principal(s). They certainly can help lift the strain of "administrivia," but don't burden them with all logistical matters. They, too, are instructional leaders in their own right (Glanz, 2004a). Rely on them to assist you in instructional leadership. Cultivate connections with key district office instructional specialists. Indeed, cultivate experienced teachers on your faculty as supporters of instructional leadership. Empowering others will provide you with some time for reflection.

Here are a few guidelines that might help you evaluate yourself:

> "It is the supreme art of the teacher to awaken joy in creative expression and knowledge."
>
> —Albert Einstein

1. Good principals take the time to reflect about what they do. They think about their failures as much as they consider their successes. They try to improve themselves by reading, attending conferences, and seeking advice from others.

2. Good principals believe and feel that they can make a difference. In the words of researchers, they have "high self-efficacy" (Sullivan, 1999). Although they may not see immediate results, they know that what they do counts.

3. Principals who show genuine and continuous interest in instruction and what teachers do in their classrooms will inspire teachers to help students achieve.

4. Good principals differentiate their supervision by providing instructional support to both novice and experienced teachers.

5. Good principals ask themselves on a daily basis, "What have I done today to make a difference to teaching and student learning?"

Reflective Questions

1. How can reflective practice help you become a more effective instructional leader? Explain.

2. How can reflective practice be used to assist teachers to improve their teaching skills?

---

2. PREPLANNING

Teachers who carefully and methodically plan and prepare for instruction are more effective than those who do not. "Organizing time and preparing materials in advance of instruction have been noted as important aspects of effective teaching" (Stronge, 2002,

p. 37). Research proves that instructional planning leads to appropriate lesson objectives, use of a variety of instructional prompts (such as advance organizers, multimedia, etc.), and higher-level questions during a lesson, in addition to minimizing student misbehavior and increasing student attention.

> *"Instruction is the lifeblood of the school."*
>
> —Gerald C. Ubben, Larry W. Hughes, and Cynthia J. Norris

Principals as instructional leaders are engaged in best practice when they spend time assisting teachers in planning lessons and instructional units. Conferencing with teachers during their prep periods about planning will increase teacher confidence and create the atmosphere that principal and teacher are instructional partners. As principal, you should review the following benefits of planning with teachers:

- Provides an overview of instruction
- Facilitates good management and instruction
- Makes learning purposeful
- Provides for sequencing and pacing
- Ties instruction with community resources
- Provides for economy of time
- Aids in reteaching and measurable learner success
- Provides for variety
- Leads to higher-level questioning
- Assists in ordering supplies
- Guides substitute teachers
- Provides documentation of instruction
- Aids in developing a repertoire of teaching strategies

Reflective Questions

1. What resources might you recommend that a teacher consult in planning a unit of instruction?

2. How would you respond to an experienced, tenured teacher who informs you that he need not plan because he is so experienced?

3. INCORPORATING ACADEMIC ALLOCATED, INSTRUCTIONAL, ENGAGED, AND SUCCESS TIME

Research into teaching effectiveness consistently points to four concepts that are critically important for promoting achievement. Effective principals work with teachers on these four concepts:

1. **Academic Allocated Time** (AAT) is the amount of time teachers assign for various subjects, such as reading, math, science, and so forth. Research studies consistently affirm strong relationships between the amount of time teachers allocate for a particular subject and student achievement. Common sense dictates that if students don't spend time learning and practicing something, then learning will suffer. As principal, you can support AAT by reviewing district and school policies with teachers and discussing subject time allocations by grade or department. However, merely allocating time is insufficient. What a teacher does with the time allocated for mathematics, for instance, is critical.

2. **Academic Instructional Time** (AIT) refers to the actual amount of time teachers spend on various subjects. Instructional time is influenced by external interruptions (such as excessive announcements over the school loudspeaker and constant interruptions from the main office, including monitors coming into class for attendance reports and the like). Minimizing these external interruptions goes far toward increasing the possibility for greater AIT. Internal factors are also significant. For instance, if teachers have difficulty controlling student behavior, AIT will be negatively affected. Therefore, to increase AIT, schools must minimize classroom interruptions, and teachers should have a system of rules and procedures that deal effectively with disciplinary problems and other disruptions. As principal, you should also develop a consistent schoolwide policy of discipline and ensure that it coincides with classroom policies.

3. **Academic Engaged Time** is the time a student actually spends attending to academic tasks. Often referred to as "time on task," this factor is most essential for promoting academic achievement. Teachers can allocate time for, say, math, and they

can spend time instructing their students in the subject, but they will not see results unless the students are *on task*. According to Ornstein (1990), "Students of teachers who provide more academic engaged time (as well as actual instructional time) learn more than students of teachers who provide relatively less time" (p. 76). Teachers who employ instructional strategies that increase time on task are more effective than those who do not. "Along with the importance of time allocated to instruction by the teacher, the time the students spend 'on-task,' or engaged in the teaching and learning activity, is an important contributor to classroom success" (Stronge, 2002, p. 48). Research verifies that teachers who engage learners use more positive reinforcement strategies, vary the types of questions they pose, address their questions to many students, tend to provide step-by-step directions to students, and come to class well prepared. As principal, you should spend a great deal of supervisory time developing strategies with teachers that increase student time on task.

4. **Academic Success Time** is the time students are successfully engaged in learning. Teachers can allocate time, provide instructional time, and ensure on-task behavior, but are students successfully on task? How do good teachers ensure that students remain successfully on task? Here are some suggestions you might share with teachers:

(a) During student independent work, spot-check by circulating around the room providing situational assistance.

(b) At times, administer a quiz (verbal or written).

(c) Call on nonvolunteers to ascertain attention and comprehension.

(d) Implement the discipline plan with consistency.

(e) Use cooperative learning grouping (see below).

(f) Group students who have specific problems in a content area.

(g) Constantly remind students to stay on task.

(h) Reward on-task behavior.

(i) Make lessons appealing.

(j) Meet the needs of all students by providing equal attention to all.

Reflective Questions

1. What can you do as the principal to ensure that each of the concepts discussed in this section is attended to in the classroom?

2. What specific strategies can you employ to improve AIT?

4. USING WAIT TIME

One of the most important teaching strategies I look for when I observe teachers is proper use of wait time. Research indicates that effective use of wait time is a major factor in promoting student learning. Wait time is an instructional strategy that refers to the amount of time students have to think during questioning. Research indicates that providing between 7 and 10 seconds for students to think before the instructor answers a question or calls on someone else improves students' accurate participation.

> "Learning does not occur in any enduring fashion unless it is sparked by people's own ardent interest and curiosity."
>
> —Peter Senge

Benefits include the following (see http://med.fsu.edu/education/FacultyDevelopment/notesbackofroom.asp):

1. Length of student responses increases.

2. Student-initiated and appropriate responses increase.

3. Student failure to respond is reduced.

4. Student confidence in responding is increased.

5. Student speculative responses increase.

6. Student-to-student interactions increase, and teacher-focused instruction decreases.

7. Student evidence to support statements increases.

8. The number of student questions increases.

9. Participation of "slow" students increases.

10. The variety of student responses increases.

Here's how I use wait time: I pose a question. I don't call on anyone until about 7 seconds have passed, even if someone raises a hand immediately. I allow think time. What happens if after 7 seconds no one responds? I ask myself, "Do I need to rephrase the question?" If so, I do so and start again. If not, I ask them to pair and share thoughts about possible answers. I give them about 60–90 seconds. This technique always yields results. Students give their answers. Not always, however, are the answers right, but at least students had time to reflect and respond. I suggest that teachers try to consciously use wait time to determine its impact on student learning.

Reflective Questions

1. What can you do as the principal to ensure that wait time is employed by teachers?

2. How might you model effective use of wait time?

---

5. USING DIRECT TEACHING

Research indicates that too much classroom time is spent on non–teaching-related activities. As principal, you must ensure that teachers spend as much time as possible in direct teaching. Monitoring direct-teaching practices in the classroom and providing supervisory workshops on strategies to increase direct teaching are essential. Effective instructional leaders reinforce these simple yet essential steps to direct teaching:

1. Begin lesson with a review of relevant previous learning and a preview of the upcoming lesson.

2. Present material in small steps, with clear and detailed explanations, and encourage students to practice after each step.

3. Ask questions and check for understanding. (Don't just ask, "Do you understand?" Actually check by calling on a nonvolunteer, by having students raise a thumb if they understand and lower it if they don't, etc.)

4. Provide systematic feedback and corrections.

5. Supervise independent practice and monitor seatwork.

6. Provide weekly or monthly review and testing.

7. Use signaling (e.g., thumbs-up).

Reflective Questions

1. What can you do as the principal to ensure that direct teaching occurs?

2. Describe a specific instructional strategy you might employ to reinforce direct teaching?

---

6. INCORPORATING LITERACY STRATEGIES

Effective teaching occurs when literacy is actively taught. The five strategies below are based on the work of Fisher, Frey, and Williams (2002). Use the information below in a professional development workshop with teachers:

Read-Alouds: I believe that reading to students should not be an activity reserved for the early-childhood grades but that students in all grades through high school benefit immeasurably from read-alouds or shared reading. Select a book that the students will enjoy, and set aside a time each day to read to them (between 5 and 20 minutes).

1. Students can listen, read along, or respond to questions prepared in advance on a worksheet or on the chalkboard. Involve them in peer whispering reading.

2. Ask questions from time to time, but avoid using this time to "test" students. Allow them the opportunity to simply "listen."

3. After each book is completed, encourage students to develop some sort of project based on the book. Allow them complete freedom to express their thoughts and ideas. If

students prefer not to do anything, that's OK. Reward students who do develop projects by posting their work in appropriate settings and venues.

Graphic Organizers: Graphic organizers provide students with visual information that extends class discussions or work with texts.

1. Encourage all students, especially visual learners, to demonstrate their understanding of a particular topic by visually presenting their thoughts and ideas.

2. Provide them homework and testing options to draw or depict in any way they choose that they have learned the material.

Vocabulary Instruction: Regardless of the content taught, teaching vocabulary is important.

1. Keep a section of the chalkboard titled, for example, "Our New Words."

2. Encourage students to record all words they do not understand. At the same time, when a new vocabulary word is encountered in class, write the word on the board. Assign students to be scribes.

3. Review each day the newly learned words.

4. Use role plays, storytelling, or any other nontraditional way to help students use the newly learned words in context.

5. Avoid at all costs the traditional ways of reviewing words, including writing them countless times, learning to spell them, writing them in sentences devoid of context, and so forth.

Writing to Learn: Encourage students to write, even in small amounts.

1. Allow class time for writing activities.

2. Encourage journal-writing time.

3. Utilize "Minute Papers," in which students use class time to record, for instance, what they have just learned or questions they still have.

Reciprocal Teaching: Many forms of this very important teaching strategy can be used. I have found reciprocal teaching particularly effective during and after learning content-laden material.

1. After some time of having presented relatively difficult material, tell students to close their notebooks and texts to find a partner to "pair and share."

2. Inform students that one of them should be designated "Student A" and the other "Student B."

3. Let Student B tell Student A everything he or she just learned. Student A cannot ask any questions. Student A simply records information. As Student B relates the information, Student A pays attention to any errors or omissions.

4. After about 5 minutes, tell Student A to tell Student B any errors or omissions. Allow about 3 minutes.

5. Tell students to now open their notebooks and texts to determine if the information they related to each other is correct.

6. Share experience with whole class.

Reflective Questions

1. How might the literacy information in this section help you as an instructional leader?

2. Describe a specific instructional strategy you might employ to reinforce literacy strategies?

---

7. DIFFERENTIATING INSTRUCTION

Classrooms are more complex and inclusive than ever. Teachers must learn how to differentiate instruction, that is, to accommodate the learning needs of all students. "Effective teachers tend to recognize individual and group differences among their students and accommodate those differences in their instruction" (Stronge, 2002, p. 57). Here are a few suggestions that might be proffered to teachers:

> *"We are committed to instructional excellence and we support the aspirations of teachers everywhere to give each boy and girl a quality school experience during the crucial years of childhood."*
>
> —From *The Principal's Creed,* National Association of Elementary School Principals

1. Utilize homogeneous grouping: Once you have identified above-average learners, provide them opportunities to work with students of similar abilities on special activities and projects.

2. Utilize their talents through peer tutoring: Train and allow these accelerated learners to assist "slower" (different) learners in specific learning activities. Students receiving the assistance will benefit, but so too will the advanced learners. They will benefit emotionally because they are helping fellow students. You are teaching them that all students are unique and should be valued. They, too, will learn the material better. I always say that if you want to really understand something, teach. These arguments in favor of peer tutoring can be shared with resistant parents who insist that such an activity detracts from the educational experiences of their children.

3. Provide enrichment activities and individualized attention: Do not ignore these accelerated learners by teaching to the "middle." Plan specific lessons for their needs. Plan on meeting and working with them individually.

4. Use cooperative learning: Research indicates that teachers who incorporate cooperative learning strategies promote student achievement.

Reflective Questions

1. What is a specific instructional strategy you might employ to reinforce the use of differentiated instruction in the classroom?

(Continued)

> 2. Cooperative learning was mentioned but was not explained in much detail. What additional information would you need to know about cooperative learning so that you could intelligently discuss the strategy with teachers and others?

8. USING DIVERGENT QUESTIONING TECHNIQUES

Good teaching cannot occur without teachers posing thought-provoking questions during lessons. Using divergent questions encourages student thinking. Note the differences between the two types of thinking below (see, e.g., http://honolulu.hawaii.edu/intranet/committees/FacDevCom/guidebk/teachtip/askquest.htm).

Convergent	Divergent
Where did the Korean War start?	Why did the Korean War start?
What are four products of Israel?	How does computer chip production in Israel affect computer export prices in our country?
Who wrote *A Tale of Two Cities?*	How does Dickens contrast the experiences of the rich and poor?
Which planet is closest to the sun?	How would you compare living conditions on Mercury with Earth?
What are the two elements of hydrogen?	How is hydrogen made?
What is the definition of a quadrilateral?	How have quadrilaterals influenced architecture?

Reflective Questions

1. What's the difference between convergent and divergent questions, and how might you employ this information to promote instructional leadership?

2. Benjamin Bloom developed the Taxonomy of Educational Objectives, in which he differentiated among six levels of thinking. How might you learn more about Bloom's levels? How do his levels relate to the use of promoting use of good questioning in the classroom?

9. SEEING TEACHING IN ACTION

Use the following list as a reflective activity with teachers (http://web.uvic.ca/terc/new_faculty/briefguide_teaching_beha viours.html):

1. **What do you do with your hands?** Gesture? Keep them in your pockets? Hold onto the podium? Play with the chalk? Hide them so students won't see them shake?

2. **Where do you stand or sit?** Behind the podium? On the table?

3. **When do you move to a different location?** Never? At regular 10-second intervals? When you change topics? When you need to write something on the board or overhead? When you answer a student's question? At what speed do you move? Do you talk and move at the same time?

4. **Where do you move?** Back behind the podium? Out to the students? To the blackboard?

5. **Where do your eyes most often focus?** On your notes? On the board or overhead? Out the window? On a spot on the wall in the back of the classroom? On the students? Could you tell who was in class today without having taken role?

6. **What do you do when you finish one content segment and are ready to move on to the next?** Say, "OK"? Ask if there are any student questions? Erase the board? Move to a different location? Make a verbal transition?

7. **When do you speak louder or softer?** When the point is very important? When nobody seems to understand? When nobody seems to be listening?

8. **When do you speak faster or slower?** When an idea is important and you want to emphasize it? When you are behind where you ought to be on the content? When students are asking questions you're having trouble answering?

9. **Do you laugh or smile in class?** When? How often?

10. **How do you use examples?** How often do you include them? When do you include them?

11. **How do you emphasize main points?** Write them on the board or overhead? Say them more than once? Ask the students if they understand them? Suggest ways they might be remembered?

12. **What do you do when students are inattentive?** Ignore them? Stop and ask questions? Interject an anecdote? Point out the consequences of not paying attention? Move out toward them?

13. **Do you encourage student participation?** How? Do you call on students by name? Do you grade participation? Do you wait for answers? Do you verbally recognize quality contributions? Do you correct student answers? On a typical day, how much time is devoted to student talk?

14. **How do you begin and end class?** With a summary and a conclusion? With a preview and a review? With a gasp and a groan? With a bang and a whimper?

Reflective Questions

1. How might you use the information in this section with teachers?

2. How does this information relate to our discussion of best practices in teaching?

---

10. LEARNING BY DOING

Simply and concisely stated, we all learn best by doing. Teachers must be encouraged to engage students in meaningful, active learning experiences. John Dewey (1899) said that people learn best "by doing." Hands-on instructional tasks encourage students to become actively involved in learning. Active learning is a pedagogically sound teaching method for any subject. Active learning increases students' interest in the material, makes the material covered more meaningful, allows students to refine their understanding of the material, and provides opportunities to relate the material to broad contexts.

Constructivist learning theory supports the idea that "hands-on" activities are essential in teaching any subject (Twomey Fosnet, 1996). According to constructivist theory, people learn best when they are given opportunities to construct meanings on their own. How best to accomplish this lofty goal becomes paramount. Simply leaving students "on their own" is a wholly inefficient and ineffective way of stimulating reflective thinking. Teachers *must* guide students and provide thought-provoking questions or frameworks as they engage in these hands-on activities.

> "But teaching is also . . . an intellectual, cultural, and contextual activity that requires skillful decisions about how to convey subject matter knowledge, apply pedagogical skills, develop human relationships, and both generate and utilize local knowledge."
>
> —Marilyn Cochran-Smith

Reflective Questions

1. How might you encourage hands-on learning in a classroom in which teaching seems to be occurring primarily through teacher lecture?

2. How might you model constructivist learning theory as an instructional leader?

CONCLUSION

This chapter has certainly not covered all there is to know about best practices in teaching. The 10 major concepts, though, provide a good start and serve as a sound basis for engaging teachers in instructional dialogue. You, as the principal, must be wary about looking for prescribed teaching behaviors as the sole criteria to assess good teaching. I am certainly not advocating that you take each of the components described in this chapter and use them to create a checklist to determine the degree to which teachers are implementing them in the classroom. The teaching ideas in this chapter are meant to serve as a means for discussion in order to assist teachers in reflecting about what they are doing instructionally in the classroom. For instance, many of us use wait time incorrectly. We pose a question and call almost immediately on the first student who raises his or her hand. Once a teacher realizes she doesn't give enough time for students to think about the question, she can then engage you in discussion about the importance of wait time. An instructional leader, at her or his best, engages teachers in reflective, nonjudgmental dialogue for the purpose of improving teaching and student learning (see Chapter 3 for a more thorough discussion of supervision).

For a variety of reasons, too many principals, from my experience, avoid instructional dialogue with teachers. Most of "principal-teacher talk" centers on sharing school or district news (even gossip), the latest district mandates and how best to implement them, student behavior problems, and "small talk" around non-school matters. How often do you find principals and teachers talking seriously, profoundly, and continuously about some aspect of the instructional program? In my view, principals who feel comfortable about instruction will take the initiative to engage teachers "all the time" in instructional dialogue. It would be refreshing to hear corridor or schoolyard principal-teacher talk center on proper use of wait time, alternative ways to differentiate instruction, and so forth.

Another important point in this context involves the all-too-common approach of minimizing teaching into small, measurable, checklist-type behaviors. Influenced in large part by national currents to standardize curriculum and recent calls for greater accountability via high-stakes testing, some principals prescribe standardized curricula and then spot-check to ensure that teachers are complying with local or state mandates. Many fear that the "deskilling" of teaching, the overemphasis on high-stakes testing, and efforts by administrators to thwart creative teaching approaches will further erode public confidence and support of education (Amrein & Berliner, 2003). Thomas Nelson (2003), editor of the *Teacher Education Quarterly*, recently lamented the trend for "people in power who are clearly not experts in the field of education . . . to control . . . what content is deemed appropriate and how that content is to be taught" (p. 3). He continues:

> To believe that all students should be learning the same material in the same way at the same time (as seen in teachers using formula-based curriculum scripts written by others),

taught by teachers who are prepared under the same exact standards (which are minimal at best), is to believe in the end of a truly public education system. (Nelson, 2003, p. 4)

There have always been those who wish to standardize teaching and view learning in the narrowest sense. Unfortunately, many educators, in particular, have not learned from the recent and distant past. Teaching cannot be standardized or reduced into ready-made recipes or prescriptions (Chomsky, 2002). Teaching is a highly complex and contextual intellectual activity that challenges and engages learners with concrete experiences, intellectual discourse, and reflective thought. Qualified principals and teachers understand that knowledge is temporary, socially constructed, culturally mediated, and developmental. From such a constructivist perspective, learning becomes a self-regulated process whereby students resolve their own cognitive conflicts with the keen guidance of teachers (Foote, Vermette, & Battaglia, 2001; Mintrop, 2002; Rodgers, 2002). Apparently those individuals who call for accountability and favor high-stakes testing do not appreciate the complexities of teaching and learning (Neill, 2003; O'Day, 2002). Measuring student learning simplistically by relying predominantly on scores gleaned from standardized tests, for instance, relegates teachers to mere technicians who simply deliver content to students.

I am certainly not against raising expectations for student learning and improving teaching practice in the classroom. Setting standards for performance and even using standardized tests as one measure, among many others, are warranted. Also warranted are efforts to weed out incompetent teachers. Teacher and school autonomy indeed must be earned by successful performance. More serious, though, are the problems generated by those who misuse and abuse results from standardized tests and attempt to lay declines in reading and math scores on the shoulders of teachers and those who train them. These individuals do not understand the complexity of teaching and educational reform (Anyon, 1997).

Finally, we must ask ourselves, "What is good teaching?" Good teaching is much more than being able to use wait time correctly and being knowledgeable about ways to differentiate instruction. Be careful not to rely solely on the 10 major ideas discussed in this chapter as *the* measures of good teaching. Good teaching, probably above all else, entails those immeasurable qualities such as caring, commitment, enthusiasm, and empathy (see, e.g., Hare, 1993). Education is much more than transmitting some set of prescribed cultural, societal, or institutional values and ideas. Education is an ongoing, spirited engagement of self-understanding and discovery (Glanz, 2004b). Etymologically, the word *education* comes from the Latin root *educare,* meaning "to draw out" or "to lead." That is, in fact, our goal as educators—to draw out that unique latent potential within each student . . . and within each teacher.

Extraordinary times call for extraordinary teachers and principals. We need teachers and principals who can challenge others to excellence, teachers and principals who love what they do. We need principals who help teachers help students achieve their potential, principals who help teachers help students understand why and how to treat others with respect, dignity, and compassion.

Haim Ginott (1993) made the point that education is more than teaching knowledge and skills in dramatic fashion when he related a message sent by a principal to his teachers on the first day of school:

> Dear Teacher:
> I am a survivor of a concentration camp. My eyes saw what no man should witness:
> Gas chambers built by learned engineers.
> Children poisoned by educated physicians.
> Infants killed by trained nurses.
> Women and babies shot and burned by high school and college graduates.
> So, I am suspicious of education.
> My request is: Help your students become human. Your efforts must never produce learned monsters, skilled psychopaths, educated Eichmanns.
> Reading, writing, arithmetic are important only if they serve to make our children more humane. (quoted in Ginott, 1993, p. 317)

Principals as instructional leaders should keep this letter handy in order to inspire and encourage good teaching that supports Ginott's ideals.

CHAPTER THREE

Best Practices in Curriculum

"Each leader is responsible for ensuring that the students entrusted to his or her care receive a first-class education in all of the core curriculum areas."

—Rod Paige

Instructional leadership is about encouraging best practices in curriculum. To do so requires you, as principal, to become familiar with basic concepts involved in curriculum development. It doesn't mean you need to become a curriculum expert, however. Successful instructional leaders facilitate best practices in curriculum in the following ways, among others:

- Model best practice in curriculum as you, the principal, review all instructional resources and materials in various content areas (e.g., reading and mathematics).
- Align teaching with curriculum.
- Encourage teachers and others to review curriculum guidelines and recommend revisions to the instructional program.
- Integrate local, state, or national standards into curriculum and instruction.
- Review testing and assessment procedures.

- Invite curriculum specialists from within and outside of the school to help facilitate curriculum revisions and development.

The following boxed material summarizes the curriculum ideas highlighted in this chapter. The list is not exhaustive but is merely meant to highlight some key concepts and ideas that successful instructional leaders should know about as they engage in curricular matters. Brief reflective activities follow each major concept to provoke thought on ways to implement or further understand each idea.

What You Should Know About Curriculum

- **The Curriculum Development Process**—"involves analysis, design, implementation, and evaluation of educational experiences in a school in order to establish goals, plan experiences, select content, and assess outcomes of school programs" (Wiles & Bondi, 1998, p. 12).
- **Tripod View of Curriculum**—involves three ways of conceiving curriculum: based on the needs of the learner, needs of society, or the knowledge base.
- **Essentialism, Progressivism, and Constructivism**—are three approaches or philosophies to guide curriculum development.
- **The Tyler Model**—involves four steps to consider in developing curriculum (one model among many others).
- **Planning, Implementing, and Assessing Teaching Learning**—involves a three-step curriculum framework.
- **Designing Quality Curriculum**—involves three guidelines offered by Glatthorn (2000) for designing quality curriculum.
- **Using Curriculum Standards**—involves attending to local, state, professional, and national standards to ensure quality learning.

---

1. UNDERSTAND THE IMPORTANCE OF CURRICULUM, AND ASSESS YOUR KNOWLEDGE OF CURRICULUM

Curriculum development is a dynamic, interactive, and complex process that serves as the foundation for good teaching practice.

Principals, as instructional leaders, must be actively involved in curriculum leadership. Such curriculum leadership is even more critical today because of national, state, and local attention to standards. For the foreseeable future, principals will continue to be pressured to respond to the national movement toward standards-based education, including high-stakes testing, by raising standards and promoting uniformity of curricular offerings to raise student academic achievement. This chapter provides some suggestions for principals in implementing standards-based curricular reform. But first, assess your basic knowledge with the following questionnaire. The remainder of this chapter will address each of the statements that follow:

Respond

SA = Strongly Agree ("For the most part, yes.")

 A = Agree ("Yes, but . . .")

 D = Disagree ("No, but . . .")

SD = Strongly Disagree ("For the most part, no.")

SA   A   D   SD   1. I see my role as principal to provide leadership in implementing state and district standards.

SA   A   D   SD   2. I have a firm understanding of basic curriculum theory.

SA   A   D   SD   3. I understand the connection between the purpose of education and curriculum development.

SA   A   D   SD   4. I cannot help teachers in areas of curriculum, because I am chiefly a manager good at administration, not curriculum.

SA   A   D   SD   5. The knowledge base or content of a curriculum is more important than the needs of the learner.

SA	A	D	SD	6.	I am a progressive curriculum thinker and doer who believes in constructivist thought and practice.
SA	A	D	SD	7.	I know how to implement the Tyler Rationale.
SA	A	D	SD	8.	I can lead teachers in developing curriculum.
SA	A	D	SD	9.	I work with teachers on an ongoing basis to develop new ways to create meaningful curricula.
SA	A	D	SD	10.	I fully understand the history of standards-based reform initiatives in this country.

Reflective Questions

1. Provide a rationale for why you must be involved in curriculum development. Make believe a teacher questions your involvement. How would you respond?

2. What else would you need to know about curriculum development?

---

2. UNDERSTAND THE THREE TYPES OF CURRICULUM

Principals should help teachers distinguish among three types of curriculum: the taught, learned, and tested. Ideally, a logical and meaningful relationship exists among these three aspects of curriculum. Teachers in class every day involve students in meaningful lessons in various content areas. They teach students about ancient Greece, algebraic equations, geologic formations, and poetry. Content may derive from prescribed curriculum guides or from an interplay of these guides and homegrown ideas. Although "taught," how do teachers ensure that curriculum is learned? Meeting the instructional needs of students by considering student involvement in curriculum or lesson

> *"Be instructional leaders as well as operational leaders."*
>
> —Elaine L. Wilmore

planning may go a long way to ensuring that learning takes place. Teachers develop traditional and nontraditional means of assessment procedures to determine the extent to which students have learned.

Principals play a key role in engaging teachers in discussion about curriculum. They can ask, "What is curriculum?" and "How can we take ownership of what is taught?" In doing so, they encourage teachers to become stakeholders in curriculum development so that teachers can enrich the educational lives of their students through meaningfully relevant pedagogy.

A key ingredient to empowering teachers to think about curriculum as an engaging instructional process is to help them explore their beliefs and values regarding education itself. Principals can ask their teachers, "Where should our emphasis be placed when developing curriculum for our students—on knowledge itself, on the learner, or on what society deems most important?" The Tripod View of Curriculum (Figure 3.1) is important to

Figure 3.1   Tripod View of Curriculum

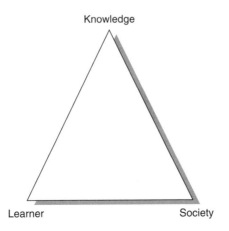

uncover fundamental beliefs of teachers and others in designing and developing curricula.

Reflective Question

1. How does the tripod figure assist in curriculum development? [Hint: Figure 3.1 depicts three emphases or sources in thinking about curriculum: subject matter (knowledge) considerations, learners' needs, and society's values. Which would you emphasize most? Is "knowledge" or subject matter most essential? In other words, should instruction be guided by subject matter considerations rather than by societal or learner needs? Should the needs of learners play the most prominent role in designing curriculum? What happens if the knowledge selected meets learner interests but does not meet societal expectations? Can you think of instances in which societal expectations drive curriculum?]

---

3. UNDERSTAND THE THREE APPROACHES TO CURRICULUM

Three main philosophies or approaches to viewing curriculum relate to each of the three aforementioned curriculum emphases: essentialism, progressivism, and constructivism. The essentialist philosophy is based on the premise that curriculum is timeless and students pursue basic truths. Essentialists believe that the school's main purpose is to cultivate content mastery in order to stimulate intellectual development. The cultivation and accumulation of knowledge for knowledge's sake is of great importance to an essentialist. What is most essential, put simply, is knowledge. Essentialist curricula stress the basic academic disciplines (liberal arts areas as well as science, mathematics, etc.).

Progressivism is a second approach to looking at curriculum. Promulgated by John Dewey (Cremin, 1964), progressivism emphasizes learning as an active process in which all students participate. Cooperative learning and problem-solving approaches are prioritized. Constructivism is aligned with progressive thinking. Constructivism is not a theory about teaching and learning per se; rather, it is a theory about the nature of knowledge itself. Knowledge is seen as temporary, developmental, socially constructed, culturally mediated, and nonobjective. Learning, then, becomes a self-regulated process wherein the individual resolves cognitive conflicts while engaged in concrete experiences, intellectual discourse, and critical reflection (Foote et al., 2001; Rodgers, 2002).

> *"If schools are to be regarded as learning communities, everyone in a school must engage in the study of what constitutes learning."*
>
> —Pam Robbins and Harvey Alvy

The principles of constructivist paradigms support the view of educators as informed decision makers. Accordingly, learning is seen as a socially mediated process in which learners construct knowledge in developmentally appropriate ways, and real learning requires that learners use new knowledge and apply what they have learned (Bransford, Brown, & Cocking, 1999; Vygotski, 1986). These beliefs emphasize "minds-on" learning. This endorses the belief that all learners must be intellectually engaged in the learning process by building on their previous knowledge and experiences and applying their new learning in meaningful contexts. To become a constructivist (mediator of learning), the teacher preparation candidate must be guided by the development of the child, motivation, and learning. Thus, central to expert instruction is a deep understanding of child development and a broad knowledge of the principles of pedagogy that serve as the blueprint for design of instruction that leads to student learning.

The third philosophy or approach to curriculum emphasizes the interests of society as most important in developing curriculum. Knowledge is important, according to this view, only to the extent to which it allows societal goals to be accomplished. Learners are expected to achieve content mastery over material deemed necessary by society. National and state standards are manifestations of societal expectations.

The Tripod View of Curriculum and its curricular approaches (see Table 3.1) are not necessarily either-or propositions. The three curricular emphases should come into play when undertaking any sort of curriculum development. Focusing on student needs and interests through a deep appreciation and understanding of child development comes into play in developing curriculum. At the same time, drawing learning experiences from broad-based discipline-centered curriculum adds legitimacy and substance to

Table 3.1   Relationship Between Three Curricular Emphases and
Three Curricular Approaches

	Knowledge	*Learner*	*Society*
Essentialism	X		
Progressivism		X	
Constructionism			X

any curriculum. Societal needs and interests must be considered in order to provide students with educational experiences and training that are useful so that students learn the fundamentals for various career choices.

Reflective Question

1. How does Table 3.1 assist in curriculum development?

---

4. UNDERSTAND AND USE THE TYLER MODEL TO DEVELOP CURRICULUM

In working with teachers to plan for teaching and learning, several curriculum models may serve as guides. One of the most helpful curriculum development models for teachers to easily implement is the one developed by Ralph Tyler (1949). His model is practical in the sense that principals can work with teachers to establish curriculum goals that can then be translated into instructional objectives. Through curriculum development, teachers identify learning activities to provide students with meaningful learning experiences.

Widely known as the Tyler Rationale, this useful model identifies four steps in curriculum development:

1. What educational purposes should the school seek to promote?

2. What educational experiences can be provided that are likely to promote these purposes?

Best Practices in Curriculum   41

3. How can these educational experiences be effectively organized?

4. How can we determine whether these purposes are being fulfilled?

Tyler (1949) advocated detailed attention to these four questions in developing curriculum. The basic idea to keep in mind about Tyler's model is that four steps are involved whenever you develop curriculum: First, state your objectives. According to Tyler, objectives must be stated in behavioral terms so that teachers can assess the extent of student learning. For example, you may state that "the student will be able to identify four of five reasons why the Civil War started." Therefore, if a student can identify only two reasons, you know that the student has not achieved the objective and needs additional work. Second, select learning activities. After objectives are articulated, select meaningfully relevant activities to help students accomplish the stated objectives. These learning activities should relate to the developmental stage of the student and should consider student needs and interests. Providing learning activities that motivate students is critical. Third, organize the learning activities. Learning activities should be concrete and sequential (i.e., one builds on the other). Learning experiences also must be well integrated, according to Tyler. That is, they should relate to each other so that students see some rhyme and reason in the activities themselves and in how they relate to the objectives. Fourth, develop a means of evaluation. You should develop performance measures to determine the extent of student learning. These may take the form of traditional testing (e.g., objectives tests) or alternate forms of assessment, although Tyler focused more on traditional means of evaluation. Additional information about Tyler's approach to curriculum may be obtained by conducting a quick Google search and typing in "Tyler Rationale." Although other models exist, and some scholars criticize Tyler's narrow view of curriculum, his model is a good and practical starting point.

Reflective Question

1. How might the Tyler model assist in curriculum development?

5. UNDERSTAND THE CURRICULUM DEVELOPMENT PROCESS

Principals can facilitate three key curriculum development steps for teachers:

1. Planning for teaching and learning

2. Implementing the plan

3. Assessing teaching and learning

According to Beach and Reinhartz (2000), "These three steps provide a framework for supervisors to use in working with teachers in groups or individually as they develop a blueprint for teaching and learning in classrooms and schools" (p. 199). Figure 3.2 illustrates the three steps of the curriculum development process. The steps are cyclical, because the process begins and ends with planning. Units or lessons are modified and improved through this process.

Developing curriculum at the planning stage involves determining prior knowledge and skills of learners, establishing instructional outcomes, and reviewing appropriate resources and materials. As teachers and principals plan together at this stage, they reflect on the teaching and learning process. During a grade conference, for example, teachers and principal can examine mandated curricula but still be free to develop and match instructional objectives with learner needs and abilities. Curricular modifications at this stage are possible and indeed recommended to plan for the most meaningful unit of instruction possible. Instructional practices, for instance, in an inclusive classroom will differ dramatically from a more homogeneous grouping of students. During this stage, teachers and principal can review availability of appropriate resources and materials that support instruction. During this stage, teachers and principal address possible teaching strategies and activities, goals and objectives, assessment procedures (always keeping the end in mind), content or subject matter, and standards that must be met. Principals play a key role in this opening step of the curriculum development process as they challenge and lead teachers to consider:

Figure 3.2 Operationalizing the Steps in Developing the Curriculum

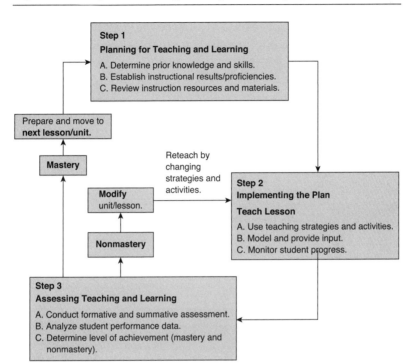

SOURCE: From Don M. Beach & Judy Reinhartz. *Supervisory Leadership: Focus on Instruction*, Published by Allyn & Bacon, Boston, MA. Copyright © 2000 by Pearson Education. Reprinted by permission of the publisher.

- Content matched to the developmental level of students
- Prerequisite knowledge and skills before undertaking a new unit of instruction
- Inductive and deductive teaching approaches
- Selection and appropriateness of learning experiences
- Sequencing of learning experiences
- Selection and appropriateness of assessment instruments

Beach and Reinhartz (2000) remind us that "the success of the curriculum depends on the quality of planning and the decisions that teachers make as they prepare for instruction" (p. 201).

During the second step of the curriculum development process, plans are implemented. Teaching is the process of implementing curricular plans. Curriculum and teaching are conceived as very much interrelated. During this step, teachers present their lessons using appropriate and varied strategies and activities. Teachers also model skills and monitor student progress (see Figure 3.2).

The third step of assessing teaching and learning is critically important. If students are not learning, the curriculum development process requires modifications. Perhaps instructional objectives need reconsideration, teaching strategies may need revision, or reteaching and review may be necessary. You can assist teachers by engaging them in informal and formal conversations about units of instruction. You can assist teachers in gathering learning data from a variety of sources beyond the traditional pencil-and-paper test. Alternative forms of assessment are shared with teachers; these may include, among other possibilities, student portfolios that include work samples and journal writing.

Reflective Question

1. How might Figure 3.2 assist in curriculum development?

---

6. UNDERSTAND HOW TO DEVELOP QUALITY CURRICULUM

Glatthorn (2000, pp. 11–12) highlights several guidelines for developing quality curriculum, some of which are reviewed below:

1. Structure the curriculum to allow for greater depth and less superficial coverage. Teachers should engage students in meaningful and detailed lessons that involve problem-solving projects and activities and critical-thinking teaching strategies. Such activities and strategies form the basis for any topic to be covered during the course of the school year. Rather than rushing to "cover" topics or "teaching for the test," teachers should give students the problem-solving and critical-thinking skills that they, on their own, can apply to any topic.

2. Structure and deliver the curriculum so that it facilitates the mastery of essential skills and knowledge of the subjects. Providing students a rich and deep knowledge base is primary, but this should be incorporated with problem-solving strategies that are realistic and meaningful to students.

3. Structure the curriculum so that it is closely coordinated. Coordinating content within lessons and among units over the course of the school year is imperative so that curriculum is sequential and well organized.

4. Emphasize both the academic and the practical. Relating content to the lived experiences of students is important to increase student learning. Hands-on activities, when feasible, are very much warranted.

Reflective Question

1. How might these guidelines assist in curriculum development?

---

7. UNDERSTAND AND USE CURRICULUM STANDARDS

Increased interest in state and national standards has had a profound effect on curriculum development. Principals should understand the historical context for this most current strand of standards-based reform initiatives. By doing so, you can ably assist teachers to work with mandated curricula but, at the same time, encourage them to view curriculum development as a viable, dynamic, and enriching process.

> *"Effective principals set high expectations and standards for the academic and social development of all students and the performance of adults."*
>
> —National Association of Elementary School Principals

Although a detailed historical overview is not possible here, you should be aware of the most recent national initiatives. Continuing in the tradition of standards-based education, President George W. Bush signed into law the No Child Left Behind

Act of 2001, a reauthorization of the Elementary and Secondary Education Act legislation of 1965. The purposes of the new legislation were to redefine the federal role in K–12 education and to help raise student achievement, especially for disadvantaged and minority students. Four basic principles were evident: stronger accountability for results, increased flexibility and local control, expanded options for parents, and an emphasis on teaching methods that presumably have been proven to work.

Principals need to know several facts relevant to the current interest in revising curriculum and raising standards. First, standards-based education is with us, and our success is due in large part to ensuring that we address these standards. Merely accepting state or national standards with grim resignation does not do much to lift our spirits about teaching and learning. Principals can provide strong leadership by helping teachers see standards as useful guides and opportunities to expand learning experiences. Ensuring that students are receiving instruction that meets national or state standards will increase confidence in teachers that they are preparing students in the best manner to meet expectations of a global economy. With the exploding knowledge and information ages and the rapid changes in technology, a growing demand for internationally competitive workers indicates to teachers the import of their work. Principals need to stress to teachers that as professionals they must meet demands placed on them by state and national agencies, while at the same time indicating "advantages and disadvantages of externally imposed standards" (Glatthorn, 2000, p. 5). Such honest and open discourse will empower teachers to develop effective strategies to best use and implement standards. Although content areas to be taught are specified in standards-based education, principals should remind teachers that creativity is still essential to ensure that the very best instructional practices take place. Following the three steps of curriculum development, explained in the previous section of this chapter (see Figure 3.2), goes a long way to keeping curriculum alive and engaging for both teachers and students.

Reflective Question

1. What standards (local, state, or national) inform your practice as principal?

In light of our discussion of standards and as an example of standards-based education, I have extracted below the ISTE (International Society for Technology in Education, the major association promoting good teaching and learning in technology) National Standards for Students (NETS·S). Peruse these standards to get a sense of what students are expected to know and do throughout the various grade levels. Then, see the reflection activity that follows the NETS·S.

K–12 NETS·S

NT.K-12.1 BASIC OPERATIONS AND CONCEPTS
- Students demonstrate a sound understanding of the nature and operation of technology systems.
- Students are proficient in the use of technology.

NT.K-12.2 SOCIAL, ETHICAL, AND HUMAN ISSUES
- Students understand the ethical, cultural, and societal issues related to technology.
- Students practice responsible use of technology systems, information, and software.
- Students develop positive attitudes toward technology uses that support lifelong learning, collaboration, personal pursuits, and productivity.

NT.K-12.3 TECHNOLOGY PRODUCTIVITY TOOLS
- Students use technology tools to enhance learning, increase productivity, and promote creativity.
- Students use productivity tools to collaborate in constructing technology-enhanced models, prepare publications, and produce other creative works.

NT.K-12.4 TECHNOLOGY COMMUNICATION TOOLS
- Students use telecommunications to collaborate, publish, and interact with peers, experts, and other audiences.
- Students use a variety of media and formats to communicate information and ideas effectively to multiple audiences.

NT.K-12.5 TECHNOLOGY RESEARCH TOOLS
- Students use technology to locate, evaluate, and collect information from a variety of sources.

(Continued)

- Students use technology tools to process data and report results.
- Students evaluate and select new information resources and technological innovations based on the appropriateness for specific tasks.

NT.K-12.6 TECHNOLOGY PROBLEM-SOLVING AND DECISION-MAKING TOOLS

- Students use technology resources for solving problems and making informed decisions.
- Students employ technology in the development of strategies for solving problems in the real world.

Profiles for Technology Literate Students

PERFORMANCE INDICATORS FOR TECHNOLOGY-LITERATE STUDENTS GRADES PreK–2

Prior to completion of Grade 2, students will:

1. Use input devices (e.g., mouse, keyboard, remote control) and output devices (e.g., monitor, printer) to successfully operate computers, VCRs, audiotapes, and other technologies. (1) [Numbers within parentheses reference specific NETS·S detailed above.]

2. Use a variety of media and technology resources for directed and independent learning activities. (1, 3)

3. Communicate about technology using developmentally appropriate and accurate terminology. (1)

4. Use developmentally appropriate multimedia resources (e.g., interactive books, educational software, elementary multimedia encyclopedias) to support learning. (1)

5. Work cooperatively and collaboratively with peers, family members, and others when using technology in the classroom. (2)

6. Demonstrate positive social and ethical behaviors when using technology. (2)

7. Practice responsible use of technology systems and software. (2)

8. Create developmentally appropriate multimedia products with support from teachers, family members, or student partners. (3)

9. Use technology resources (e.g., puzzles, logical thinking programs, writing tools, digital cameras, drawing tools) for problem solving, communication, and illustration of thoughts, ideas, and stories. (3, 4, 5, 6)

10. Gather information and communicate with others using telecommunications, with support from teachers, family members, or student partners. (4)

GRADES 3–5

Prior to completion of Grade 5, students will:

1. Use keyboards and other common input and output devices (including adaptive devices when necessary) efficiently and effectively. (1)

2. Discuss common uses of technology in daily life and the advantages and disadvantages those uses provide. (1, 2)

3. Discuss basic issues related to responsible use of technology and information and describe personal consequences of inappropriate use. (2)

4. Use general purpose productivity tools and peripherals to support personal productivity, remediate skill deficits, and facilitate learning throughout the curriculum. (3)

5. Use technology tools (e.g., multimedia authoring, presentation, Web tools, digital cameras, scanners) for individual and collaborative writing, communication, and publishing activities to create knowledge products for audiences inside and outside the classroom. (3, 4)

6. Use telecommunications efficiently to access remote information, communicate with others in support of direct and independent learning, and pursue personal interests. (4)

(Continued)

7. Use telecommunications and online resources (e.g., e-mail, online discussions, Web environments) to participate in collaborative problem-solving activities for the purpose of developing solutions or products for audiences inside and outside the classroom. (4, 5)

8. Use technology resources (e.g., calculators, data collection probes, videos, educational software) for problem solving, self-directed learning, and extended learning activities. (5, 6)

9. Determine which technology is useful and select the appropriate tool(s) and technology resources to address a variety of tasks and problems. (5, 6)

10. Evaluate the accuracy, relevance, appropriateness, comprehensiveness, and bias of electronic information sources. (6)

GRADES 6–8

Prior to completion of Grade 8, students will:

1. Apply strategies for identifying and solving routine hardware and software problems that occur during everyday use. (1)

2. Demonstrate knowledge of current changes in information technologies and the effect those changes have on the workplace and society. (2)

3. Exhibit legal and ethical behaviors when using information and technology, and discuss consequences of misuse. (2)

4. Use content-specific tools, software, and simulations (e.g., environmental probes, graphing calculators, exploratory environments, Web tools) to support learning and research. (3, 5)

5. Apply productivity/multimedia tools and peripherals to support personal productivity, group collaboration, and learning throughout the curriculum. (3, 6)

6. Design, develop, publish, and present products (e.g., Web pages, videotapes) using technology resources that demonstrate and

communicate curriculum concepts to audiences inside and outside the classroom. (4, 5, 6)

7. Collaborate with peers, experts, and others using telecommunications and collaborative tools to investigate curriculum-related problems, issues, and information, and to develop solutions or products for audiences inside and outside the classroom. (4, 5)

8. Select and use appropriate tools and technology resources to accomplish a variety of tasks and solve problems. (5, 6)

9. Demonstrate an understanding of concepts underlying hardware, software, and connectivity, and of practical applications to learning and problem solving. (1, 6)

10. Research and evaluate the accuracy, relevance, appropriateness, comprehensiveness, and bias of electronic information sources concerning real-world problems. (2, 5, 6)

GRADES 9–12

Prior to completion of Grade 12, students will:

1. Identify capabilities and limitations of contemporary and emerging technology resources and assess the potential of these systems and services to address personal, lifelong learning, and workplace needs. (2)

2. Make informed choices among technology systems, resources, and services. (1, 2)

3. Analyze advantages and disadvantages of widespread use and reliance on technology in the workplace and in society as a whole. (2)

4. Demonstrate and advocate for legal and ethical behaviors among peers, family, and community regarding the use of technology and information. (2)

(Continued)

5. Use technology tools and resources for managing and communicating personal/professional information (e.g., finances, schedules, addresses, purchases, correspondence). (3, 4)

6. Evaluate technology-based options, including distance and distributed education, for lifelong learning. (5)

7. Routinely and efficiently use online information resources to meet needs for collaboration, research, publications, communications, and productivity. (4, 5, 6)

8. Select and apply technology tools for research, information analysis, problem-solving, and decision-making in content learning. (4, 5)

9. Investigate and apply expert systems, intelligent agents, and simulations in real-world situations. (3, 5, 6)

10. Collaborate with peers, experts, and others to contribute to a content-related knowledge base by using technology to compile, synthesize, produce, and disseminate information, models, and other creative works. (4, 5, 6)

SOURCE: Reprinted with permission from National Educational Technology Standards for Students: Connecting Curriculum and Technology. Copyright © 2000, ISTE (International Society for Technology in Education), iste@iste.org, www.iste.org. All rights reserved. Permission does not constitute an endorsement by ISTE.

Reflective Question

1. How might you address the aforementioned ISTE NETS·S in your attempt to strengthen technology teaching?

CONCLUSION

Curriculum involves an analysis of all the learning experiences that occur in school. Effective instructional leaders involve teachers in curriculum development. Discussions ensue around implementing local or state curricular mandates and how to design the best curriculum to meet the learning needs of all students. To accomplish these important tasks requires that you have the requisite curriculum knowledge and skills. As emphasized earlier, you need not be the sole expert in curriculum. Wise principals draw upon the skills of curriculum supervisors and consultants. Still, having a basic and sound knowledge of curriculum development is essential. Knowledgeable principals are more likely to understand the constraints and challenges of curriculum development and are better able to discuss problems and issues intelligently. Good teaching does not occur in isolation of curriculum. Effective principals as instructional leaders know this fact.

Effective principals are involved in these curricular activities, among others:

- Reviewing district and state curriculum guidelines and procedures
- Discussing district and school curriculum with colleagues and district office personnel, including, first and foremost, the superintendent
- Organizing curriculum discussion groups at faculty and grade conferences with teachers
- Assigning curriculum facilitators among the faculty and assistant principals
- Reviewing instructional materials and resources
- Evaluating the relevancy of curriculum materials and resources
- Making recommendations to teacher and district office officials
- Involving, most importantly, teachers in the curriculum design and revision process
- Soliciting input from others in the curriculum process (e.g., curriculum specialists, parents, and students)
- Examining the relationship between teaching and curriculum
- Exploring the impact of the hidden curriculum on the formal curriculum
- Understanding the relationships among the formal curriculum, the hidden curriculum, the curriculum that is actually taught in the classroom, and the tested curriculum
- Assessing the impact of curriculum materials on student achievement
- Engaging teachers on a continual basis in discussion of teaching, learning, and curriculum

CHAPTER FOUR

Best Practices in Supervision and Professional Development

"Supervision is and always will be the key to the high instructional standards of America's public schools."

—Harold Spears

"The goal of supervision is to facilitate the process of teaching and learning through a multitude of approaches that can encompass curriculum and staff development, action research, and peer, self-, and student assessment. . . . Supervision is the process of engaging teachers in instructional dialogue for the purpose of improving teaching and increasing student achievement."

—Susan Sullivan and Jeffrey Glanz

"Too often, professional development is not carefully conceived to help teachers develop and use specific skills needed to increase student achievement. Also, most professional development is not rigorously evaluated to determine what

teachers learned and how effectively they applied that learning in their schools and classrooms. As educators heed the call for a research-based approach to professional development, they must redesign their programs to provide an effective system of instructional support for teachers. This new approach to professional development must be linked to concrete teaching tasks, organized around problem solving, informed by research, and sustained over time."

—Gene R. Carter

In a book devoted to principal instructional leadership, I believe that no area is more important than providing for supervision and professional development; hence, the length of this chapter. Supervision is a process that engages teachers in instructional dialogue for the purpose of improving teaching and promoting student achievement. Principals should view themselves (and be seen) as "teachers of teachers." This notion is predicated on the condition that principals have adequate teaching experience themselves and possess the knowledge and skills to communicate good teaching practice to teachers. Principals, as instructional leaders, understand how to work with teachers in order to improve teaching and promote student learning. Principals can incorporate a variety of instructional improvement strategies, including clinical supervision that incorporates purposeful classroom observation of teachers in action, not for evaluative purposes but to engage teachers in instructional dialogue about classroom practice. In fact, no discussion of evaluation is found in this book because the chief purpose of evaluation is accountability, not instructional improvement.

In identifying best practices, this chapter highlights two forms of supervision: clinical supervision and action research. Although other approaches to supervision are common (e.g., cognitive coaching, Costa & Garmston, 2002; mentoring, Reiman & Thies-Sprinthall, 1998; peer coaching, Showers & Joyce, 1996; walk-throughs, Downey, Steffy, English, Frase, & Poston, 2004, etc.), these approaches in varying degrees utilize the steps of clinical supervision. Action research, quietly emerging as a popular alternative to traditional supervision, is often teacher initiated in the sense that the teacher identifies a problem, collects and interprets data, and arrives at some conclusion to improve practice (Glanz, in press). Although the process can serve as the basis for discussion with a coach or supervisor, action research generally does not incorporate clinical supervision phases (although it can). These two approaches are identified as best practices, among others (see, e.g., Beach, 2000; Coppola, Scricca, & Connors, 2004; Glickman, Gordon, & Ross-Gordon, 2005; Pajak, 2000; Zepeda, 2003a), and are much favored over a checklist approach to supervision that is perfunctory, evaluative, and not very useful for teachers.

What You Should Know About Supervision and Professional Development

- **Clinical Supervision**—is a cyclical process of engaging teachers in instructional dialogue based on three basic stages: planning, observing, and analysis or reflection.
- **Action Research**—occurs when principals encourage teachers to think about their teaching and student learning in systematic ways by employing the scientific method: identify a question or problem, pose research questions, gather and analyze data, interpret results, derive conclusions, and take action to improve practice.
- **Professional Development**—is a process of supporting teachers' work and student learning by systematic, continuous, meaningful, knowledge-based workshops and seminars around collaboratively developed topics.
- **PCOWBIRDS**—All good principals work with teachers on instructional activities that include planning, conferences, observations, workshops, sharing bulletins and research, intervisitations, providing resources, demo lessons, and staff development.

---

1. IMPLEMENT CLINICAL SUPERVISION

Clinical supervision, as a model of supervision developed 30 years ago, grew out of the dissatisfaction with traditional educational practice and supervisory methods (see Sullivan & Glanz, 2005, Chapter 1). Robert Goldhammer (1969), one of the early progenitors of clinical supervision, stated that the model for clinical supervision was

Figure 4.1   Clinical Supervision Cycle

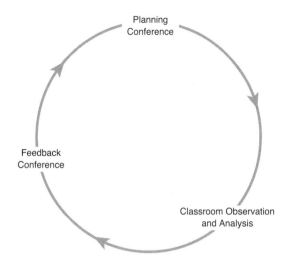

SOURCE: Glanz, *The Assistant Principal's Handbook* (2004). Corwin Press.

"motivated, primarily, by contemporary views of weaknesses that commonly exist in educational practice" (p. 1). Invented by Morris Cogan (Pajak, 2000), clinical supervision is premised on the notion that teaching could be improved by a prescribed, formal process of collaboration between teacher and supervisor. Clinical supervision focuses on the improvement of instruction by means of systematic cycles of planning, observation, and intensive intellectual analysis during a feedback conference (see Figure 4.1).

Clinical supervision is a superb means for improving teaching and promoting student learning. If you wish to serve as an instructional leader, then you should become familiar with clinical supervision. *To be effective, clinical supervision should be divorced from evaluation.* In other words, teachers must be comfortable sharing their teaching practices with principals who are trustworthy and will keep any information gleaned confidential. Clinical supervision, if it is to work, must promote instructional dialogue between you and the teacher in an open, congenial, and trusting manner. The fundamental premise of clinical supervision is to open up channels of communication; provide feedback to teachers about their teaching in an objective, nonjudgmental manner; and to dialogue about teaching and learning.

Here are some suggestions for creating a safe and comfortable environment for clinical supervision implementation:

- Never use the clinical supervision cycle for evaluative purposes. In other words, don't place an evaluation letter in a teacher's mailbox that emerged from an observation conducted after clinical supervision.
- Role-play the cycle at a faculty or grade conference in order to demonstrate its use.
- Have an experienced teacher conduct the cycle with you teaching a demonstration lesson. Have it videotaped for viewing at a faculty or grade conference.
- At every occasion, communicate your confidence in faculty and your commitment to instructional excellence and support of faculty in every way.

Before I introduce a version of the clinical supervision cycle (Sullivan & Glanz, 2000), it is important to understand that clinical supervision is not only a structure but a concept, and as such, it contains a series of assumptions. Goldhammer, Anderson, and Krajewski (1993) outlined nine major characteristics of clinical supervision that we believe are consistent with any of the approaches and structures in this book:

1. It is a technology for improving instruction.

2. It is a deliberate intervention into the instructional process.

3. It is goal oriented, combining the school's needs with the personal growth needs of those who work within the school.

4. It assumes a professional working relationship between teacher(s) and supervisor(s).

5. It requires a high degree of mutual trust, as reflected in understanding, support, and commitment to growth.

6. It is systematic, although it requires a flexible and continuously changing methodology.

7. It creates a productive (i.e., healthy) tension for bridging the gap between the real and the ideal.

8. It assumes that the supervisor knows a great deal about the analysis of instruction and learning and also about productive human interaction.

9. It requires both preservice training (for supervisors), especially in observation techniques, and continuous inservice reflection on effective approaches. (Goldhammer et al., 1993, pp. 52–53)

The Clinical Supervision Cycle

Richard Weller's (1997) formal definition of clinical supervision provides a basis upon which we can develop a cycle of supervision: "Clinical supervision may be defined as supervision focused upon the improvement of instruction by means of systematic cycles of planning, observation, and intensive intellectual analysis of actual teaching performances in the interest of rational modification" (p. 11). Weller referred to the three phases of the clinical supervision cycle as represented in Figure 4.1.

Before I begin to concisely explain each of the three steps in clinical supervision (for a fuller treatment, see Sullivan & Glanz, 2005), you should realize that the approach taken for clinical supervision depends on the developmental (Glickman, Gordon, & Ross-Gordon, 1998) level of the teacher. Three distinct approaches to working with individuals include the following:

- Directive informational
- Collaborative
- Self-directed

These approaches range from somewhat principal controlled to primarily teacher controlled. The approach the principal chooses is supposed to match the specific teacher's level of development. In reality, many of us tend to favor one approach in our interactions with others. Some supervision systems include a "directive control" approach, in which the principal makes the decision and tells the individual or group how to proceed. Although I agree that "different folks need different strokes" and that varying school circumstances call for a range of approaches, my belief that meaningful learning is dependent on the learner's involvement in constructing that knowledge eliminates the need for the directive control approach. Many principals over the years have used this approach, many continue to follow it, and you may favor it yourself. Nonetheless, I think that the collaborative and nondirective models are the most effective, with the occasional application of a modified directive informational approach.

The principal who uses the directive informational approach frames the choices for the group or individual and then asks for input. In the collaborative approach, the principal and the individual or group share information and possible solutions as equals to arrive at a mutual plan. In the third approach, the principal facilitates the individual or group in developing a self-plan or in making its own decision. Glickman et al. (1998), for example, believe that the teacher's level of development, expertise, and commitment and the nature of the situation determine the choice of approach.

The Directive Informational Approach

Key Steps—Directive Informational Approach

1. Identify the problem or goal and solicit clarifying information.

2. Offer solutions. Ask for the teacher's input into the alternatives offered, and request additional ideas.

3. Summarize chosen alternatives, ask for confirmation, and request that the teacher restate final choices.

4. Set a follow-up plan and meeting.

This approach is used primarily for new teachers or those who are experiencing difficulties that they don't have the knowledge, expertise, or confidence to resolve on their own or collaboratively. These teachers are seeking or need direction and guidance from a principal who can provide expert information and experienced guidance. Nonetheless, the principal wants the teacher to seek solutions and generate ideas so as to feel at least some ownership of the final choices. Therefore, the principal is the initiator of suggestions and alternatives. The teacher can later refine these suggestions with her or his own ideas.

1. Identify the problem or goal and solicit clarifying information.

Avoid small talk and focus immediately on the problem or goal in question. Ask the teacher for clarification of the situation so that you are both sure that you are addressing the same problem or goal.

2. Offer solutions. Ask for the teacher's input into the alternatives offered, and request additional ideas.

Even though the new teacher might feel overwhelmed, your ideas will probably stimulate his or her thinking. Offering input and requesting additional ideas will give the teacher a feeling of ownership and allow him or her to begin constructing a personal perspective. Separating the alternatives from the request for additional ideas allows the teacher to think through the suggestions and then come up with modifications or new possibilities.

3. Summarize chosen alternatives, ask for confirmation, and request that the teacher restate final choices.

Verification that both you and the teacher have the same understanding of the final choices is crucial. Two people can easily interpret the same words differently or hear different words. Therefore, if each party repeats his or her understanding, any misunderstandings or differences in perceptions can be cleared up before action is taken.

4. Set a follow-up plan and meeting.

A concrete plan (written is preferable) and a scheduled meeting are the only ways that two very busy professionals can be sure of the follow-through that is crucial to the success of any plan.

The Collaborative Approach

Key Steps—Collaborative Approach

1. Identify the problem from the teacher's perspective, soliciting as much clarifying information as possible.

2. Reflect back what you've heard for accuracy.

3. Begin collaborative brainstorming, asking the teacher for his or her ideas first.

4. Problem-solve through a sharing and discussion of options.

5. Agree on a plan and follow-up meeting.

In the collaborative approach, the goal is to resolve a problem or reach a goal through shared decision making. You should encourage the teacher to develop his or her ideas first to allow maximum ownership. Nonetheless, the brainstorming and problem solving are shared, and disagreement is encouraged, with assurances that a mutual solution will be reached. The conference always ends with a restatement of agreed-upon plans and the setting of a follow-up meeting. Unresolved issues can be included in the planning process and revisited at the follow-up session.

1. Identify the problem from the teacher's perspective, soliciting as much clarifying information as possible.

With the exception of some new teachers and those with problematic practices, you want the teacher to initiate the discussion from his or her perspective. The more information provided, the clearer the situation for both parties. Therefore, a more complete description can be drawn out with prompts, such as eye contact, encouraging open body language and nonverbal cues, paraphrasing, probing questions, and phrases such as "Tell me more," "Uh-huh," "I see," and "I understand."

2. Reflect back what you've heard for accuracy.

It is crucial that you verify that you've heard accurately the content and perspective of the teacher. A summary of what you understood, with the teacher's verification of what you heard, can avoid many misunderstandings and problems down the road. You may feel like you sound silly repeating like this; rest assured that the teacher is hanging on your every word to be sure that you heard and understood.

3. Begin collaborative brainstorming, asking the teacher for his or her ideas first.

If you propose options first, the teacher might not try and develop his or her own ideas and might simply follow what you suggested. Because the teacher is the one most familiar with the situation, it is important to allow him or her to build on that knowledge or to decide to construct a different or new resolution.

4. Problem-solve through a sharing and discussion of options.

One of the greatest challenges you have in a collaborative approach is to encourage disagreement convincingly. Few teachers are accustomed to administrators fostering challenges and encouraging risk taking. Asking for the teacher's suggestions is a first step. Promoting an open dialogue about the options is the second step.

5. Agree on a plan and follow-up meeting.

In the complex lives of teachers and administrators, a written plan for implementing agreed-upon solutions and those yet to be resolved will save a lot of time in the long run. What often seems time-consuming can be "cost-effective" in the final analysis. Taking the time to write out a plan and set up the next appointment are the essential concluding steps.

The Self-Directed Approach

Key Steps—Self-Directed Approach

1. Listen carefully to the teacher's initial statement.

2. Reflect back your understanding of the problem.

3. Constantly clarify and reflect until the real problem is identified.

4. Have the teacher problem-solve and explore the consequences of various actions.

5. Have the teacher commit to a decision and firm up a plan.

6. Restate the teacher's plan and set a follow-up meeting.

The goal of the self-directed approach is to enable the teacher to reflect on the problem, draw conclusions, and construct his or her own alternatives. You serve more as a coach who does not express his or her point of view or ideas unless the teacher specifically requests them. You function as the facilitator of the teacher's development of his or her own ideas. The outcome should always be the teacher's autonomous decision. This approach is appropriate for a very knowledgeable and experienced teacher. It also can be successful in providing a sense of ownership when the teacher is the primary person responsible for carrying out a decision or when the decision or problem at hand has limited ramifications. A less experienced but creative and promising teacher can also benefit from the guided ownership that this approach affords.

1. Listen carefully to the teacher's initial statement.

As in the collaborative approach, the starting point is the teacher's perspective of the situation. The techniques and prompts are the same as in the collaborative approach: eye contact, body language, paraphrasing, verbal cues, and probing questions.

2. Reflect back your understanding of the problem.

Again, as in the collaborative approach, verification that you have clearly and accurately understood the teacher's perspective is essential. Reflecting back what has been heard begins to accomplish this task. In addition, paraphrasing can clarify any uncertainty you may have about what has been expressed and can even allow the teacher to distance himself or herself from what was said and reflect on it from the outside.

3. Constantly clarify and reflect until the real problem is identified.

The crucial prerequisite to solving a problem is to conceptualize accurately what the problem is. Solutions often are hidden in the identification of the problem, thereby limiting the range of resolutions. Thus, the real need must be ascertained. For example, your husband says he's taking the car, but you have a meeting. Your need is not necessarily to have the car, but to find a way to get to the meeting. The facilitator's role is to use the reflecting/prompting/questioning process judiciously to permit the teacher to arrive at a crystallization of the need.

4. Have the teacher problem-solve and explore the consequences of various actions.

Once the need has been identified, simply ask the teacher to think of possible alternatives. Assist the teacher in walking through the steps, process, and consequences of each action. Ask questions such as "What would happen if . . . ?" or "How would you . . . ?" Then ask the teacher to explore the advantages and disadvantages of the alternatives. At this point, the teacher may be ready to respond to concluding questions, such as "Which do you think will work best? Why? In what ways would it be better?"

5. Have the teacher commit to a decision and firm up a plan.

Once the teacher makes a choice, you can request a plan and encourage a walk-through of the next steps. "What, who, when, how, where" or the provision of simple planning forms that the teacher can complete may be part of the plan.

6. Restate the teacher's plan and set a follow-up meeting.

It is important for you to restate the teacher's plan before ending the meeting. This verification will avoid future misunderstandings. In addition, even though the teacher owns the plan, the scheduling of a follow-up meeting to see how it's working should always conclude the session.

Table 4.1 compares and contrasts the three approaches.

With an understanding of three approaches to working with individuals, I will now present an overview of the steps of clinical supervision.

Clinical Supervision Step #1: The Planning Conference

Lauren Cardone, the newly appointed principal of Marlboro Middle School, began her first set of classroom observations as

Table 4.1 Approach Comparison

Directive Informational	*Collaborative*	*Self-Directed*
1. Supervisor identifies problem, then solicits clarifying information.	1. Supervisor seeks to identify problem from teacher's perspective.	1. Supervisor asks teacher to identify problem.
2. Supervisor offers solutions and then requests input.	2. Collaborative brainstorming for solutions.	2. Clarification and reflection until teacher identifies problem.
3. Supervisor summarizes and then asks for confirmation.	3. Problem-solve through sharing and discussion.	3. Teacher problem-solves and explores consequences.
4. Teacher restates final choices.	4. Joint agreement on plan.	4. Teacher commits to decision.

SOURCE: Sullivan/Glanz, *Supervision That Improves Teaching* (1999). Corwin Press.

early as possible in the fall. She hoped to develop trusting relationships that would permit her and the teachers to focus on the improvement of teaching and learning, and not on the bureaucratic process of evaluation. She decided to meet with and observe the newest teachers first.

Lauren set up a planning conference with a brand-new language arts teacher. She had heard that Sarah, a recent graduate of a high-quality master's program, was having difficulty implementing her student-centered practices. Some of the students had not been exposed to cooperative learning groups before, and rumor had it that some of her classes were out of control. Nonetheless, Lauren decided to query Sarah about what she felt her concerns were. To make Sarah comfortable, Lauren set up a meeting in Sarah's classroom, not in the principal's office.

"Hi, Sarah. How's it going?"

"OK, I guess."

"Since I will be beginning nontenured teacher observations, I thought we could discuss a particular area, interest, or concern that could be the focus of the observation."

"Gosh, I wouldn't know where to start. You pick it."

"I know that you use a lot of exciting, innovative teaching methods. Is there any one in particular that you'd like some feedback on?"

"Mmm . . . I've been trying to have the students work in cooperative groups to discuss their writing, and it doesn't seem to be working in some classes. I have a rambunctious seventh-grade class that doesn't work well in groups at all, and I can't seem to get control of the process. Could you sit in on that class?"

"Sure. Let me show you a couple of tools I could use to observe the groups and see which one you think might pinpoint your concerns."

They decide to use the Cooperative Learning Performance Indicator instrument (see section below) created by D. W. Johnson and R. T. Johnson (1994).

"What is a convenient time for me to visit when you will be using cooperative groups with the seventh graders?"

"How about third period next Tuesday? They're usually awake by then but not yet completely out of control."

"Fine. Next Tuesday, October 1, third period. While we're at it, could we set a time to meet after the observation? How about during your professional period the following day?"

"Sounds OK to me."

"Agreed. Third period on Tuesday and second period on Wednesday. By the way, if you have any other input that would be helpful before I visit, don't hesitate to stop in and share it with me. I'm looking forward to seeing students using this wonderful method."

Reflective Question

1. What does Lauren do to make Sarah feel relaxed and at the same time focus on instruction? How does she get Sarah to reflect on her own perceptions of her needs?

Key Steps—Planning Conference

1. Decide collaboratively the focus of the observation.

2. Determine the method and form of observation.

3. Set the time of the observation and the postconference.

The goals of the planning conference are:

- To identify teacher interests and concerns in a collaborative manner
- To clarify that the primary purpose of the observation is to improve teaching and learning
- To reduce stress and make the teacher feel comfortable about the process
- To choose an observation tool and schedule the visit and postconference

The three steps of planning conferences are:

1. Decide collaboratively the focus of the observation.
Whereas the chief purpose of the observation is to improve instruction, it is essential to have the teacher's perspective on his or her concerns and interests. Even a new teacher can help

identify the primary or most urgent concerns. Change occurs most easily if the teacher has a role in providing the focus.

2. Determine the method and form of observation.

Once the focus is determined, you can discuss the appropriate tools. You will decide whether to include the teacher in making the choice of the observation tool. A newer or less secure teacher may have enough to cope with without taking part in that decision.

3. Set the time of the observation and the postconference.

It is important, wherever possible, to provide the teacher with the opportunity to choose the day and time. The teacher knows in which class the focus that he or she has chosen can be observed best. Once he or she has had a role in deciding the focus, the choice is simplified. It becomes a learning experience with less likelihood of the visit being an occasion to put on a show.

Clinical Supervision Step #2: The Observation

The principal understands that teaching is a challenging art and science. Teaching occurs in an incredibly fast-paced environment, in which hundreds of overt and subtle interactions occur between teachers and students as well as between students and students. Given the complex nature of classroom life (Jackson, 1990), tools for systematically recording classroom interactions are especially useful to assist teachers in understanding more fully and becoming aware of classroom behavior (Good & Brophy, 1997). Principals believe that "life in classrooms" is context bound, situationally determined, and complex. The principal is not and should not be the overseer or prescriber, but rather the guide, facilitator, or collaborator. Relying on enhanced communication and shared understandings, the principal can effectively use observation instruments to encourage interpersonal and collegial relationships. This section does review all aspects of the varied observation instruments that are possible. For a fuller treatment of varied observation instruments, consult Sullivan and Glanz (2005) or Willerman, McNeely, and Koffman (1991). Let's review, though, 10 general guidelines for any classroom observation.

Ten Guidelines of Observation. Here are several guiding principles about observation that should be kept in mind:

1. Good supervision is about engaging teachers in reflective thinking and discussion based on insightful and useful observation, not on evaluation.

2. Supervision, relying on the use of observation instruments to provide teachers information about their classrooms, is likely to enhance teacher thought and commitment to instructional improvement.

3. Observation is a two-step process: first, to describe what has occurred, and then to interpret what it means.

4. Too often, we jump into what has been termed the *interpretation trap.* We jump to conclusions about a particular behavior before describing that behavior. When we interpret first, we not only lose description of that event, but also create communication difficulties that might result in teacher resistance.

5. The precise observation tool or technique should be chosen collaboratively between teacher and supervisor. However, in most cases, the teacher ultimately should determine the instrument to be used.

6. Observing a classroom is not necessarily an objective process. Personal bias should be acknowledged and discussed. Although two or more individuals may agree on what has occurred (during the description stage), they might interpret the event's meaning differently. Personal experience, beliefs, and prejudices can lead to misinterpretations. Awareness of the possibility of personal bias is the first step toward interpreting classroom behavior effectively and as objectively as possible.

7. Observing takes skill and practice. Quite often, we interpret as we observe. If these tools of observation are to be effective, then you must practice separating interpretation from description.

8. Be aware of the limitations of observation. No observer can see or notice all interactions. Attempts to do so lead only to frustration and confusion. Start observations in a limited setting with a small group, and observe one specific behavior, such as the quality of teacher questions.

9. Disclosure is an essential element for successful observation. Prior to entering the classroom, the observer should discuss with the teacher the following items: where to sit in the room, how to introduce the observer to students, and so forth.

10. Don't draw conclusions based on one observation. Teachers have "bad" days, and lessons sometimes don't work. Students, too, may have "bad" days. Multiple observations with different focuses are necessary.

I advised earlier that you consult Sullivan and Glanz (2005) for a detailed description of many different forms of quantitative and qualitative observation instruments. One interesting approach you can use, though, is videotaping and audio recording. According to Acheson and Gall (1997),

> Video and audio recordings are among the most objective observation techniques. . . . They allow teachers to see themselves as students see them. . . . [They] can pick up a great deal of what teachers and students are doing and saying. A good recording captures the "feel" of classroom interaction. (p. 111)

Videos and audios, according to Acheson and Gall, are examples of "wide lenses" that are particularly useful "in supervising teachers who are defensive or who are not yet ready to select particular teaching behaviors for improvement" (p. 107). Acheson and Gall conclude, "After reviewing wide-lens data, these teachers may be more ready to reflect on their teaching, identify specific teaching behaviors for focused observations, and set self-improvement goals" (pp. 107–108).

Research demonstrates that teachers are likely to change their instructional behaviors on their own after their classroom has been described to them by an observer. Observation is a mirror and thus a stimulus for change. Good supervision is about engaging teachers in reflective thinking and discussion based on insightful and useful observation tools and techniques. In the next section, I place these observation tools within the context of a clinical supervision program.

Clinical Supervision Step #3: The Postconference

Often eliminated, this final step is critical. Find time for this important follow-up session. If you really want to serve as an instructional leader, you will make time for this important activity. Without it, the previous two steps are nearly worthless. Teacher confidence will wane without adequate follow-up. As you begin the postconference, ask the teacher how she or he felt about the lesson. Follow one of the three approaches below, depending on the developmental level of the teacher.

Key Steps—Directive Informational Approach

1. Identify the problem or goal and solicit clarifying information.

2. Offer solutions. Ask for the teacher's input into the alternatives offered and request additional ideas.

3. Summarize chosen alternatives, ask for confirmation, and request that the teacher restate final choices.

4. Set a follow-up plan and meeting.

Key Steps—Collaborative Approach

1. Identify the problem from the teacher's perspective, soliciting as much clarifying information as possible.

2. Reflect back what you've heard for accuracy.

3. Begin collaborative brainstorming, asking the teacher for his or her ideas first.

4. Problem-solve through a sharing and discussion of options.

5. Agree on a plan and follow-up meeting.

Key Steps—Self-Directed Approach

1. Listen carefully to the teacher's initial statement.

2. Reflect back your understanding of the problem.

3. Constantly clarify and reflect until the real problem is identified.

4. Have the teacher problem-solve and explore consequences of various actions.

5. Have the teacher commit to a decision and firm up a plan.

6. Restate the teacher's plan and set a follow-up meeting.

Reflective Questions

Find a colleague with whom you can practice the three steps of clinical supervision. You play the role of the principal and set up any scenario; for example, you are observing a history lesson at the high school level for 20 minutes. Complete the clinical super-vision cycle, and prepare the following written report:

A. Summarize or recount each phase of the cycle: planning conference, observation, and postconference.

B. Analyze the data from each approach choice you made and then interpret the data.
1. How much teacher input was there in the planning confer-ence? Would you recommend a change in the approach to this teacher in another planning session? Why?
2. Did the observation tool reveal the behaviors on which you and your colleague agreed to focus? How or why not? Was the observation tool you chose appropriate and effec-tive? Is it a tool you would use again? Why or why not?
3. What was the teacher's reaction to the process?

C. Provide a final reflection on the whole process, that is, your personal evaluation of what worked and was of value, and what you will think about doing differently in the future.

---

2. ENCOURAGE ACTION RESEARCH

Principals, as instructional leaders, are responsible, first and fore-most, for promoting best teaching practice (Zepeda, 2003b). Good principals continually engage teachers in instructional dialogue and reflective practices so that they are best equipped to improve the academic performance of all their students. These principals are aware of the varied instructional strategies that aim, directly or indirectly, to improve student achievement (Ruebling, Stow, Kayona, & Clarke, 2004).

One of the neglected areas or instruments for instructional improvement is the practice of action research. Once thought of as only a tool to collect data for teachers' personal and professional development, action research today is employed by principals as cutting-edge practice that encourages teachers, as thoughtful professionals, to reflect, refine, and improve teaching. Action research, then, becomes an integral component in any instructional supervision program. Action research as instructional supervision, however, is a relatively recent phenomenon (see Glanz, in press, for a brief history of action research as supervision).

Action Research as Supervision in Practice: Two Case Studies

Doris Harrington is a tenured math teacher at Northern Valley Regional High School, a school with 1,100 students. Having taught in the school for 18 years, Doris is excited about the new program that Principal Bert Ammerman spearheaded to enhance professional development and instructional improvement. "I think it's neat that we now have a system in place in which we feel empowered. I mean, having an option, a choice in determining my professional development is certainly new and much appreciated."

Doris selects an "action research" plan as a part of the supervisory program that teachers, supervisors, and administrators collaboratively developed. "I've read so much about action research and am so excited that others now appreciate how important it is to provide time for teachers to reflect about what we do every day in the classroom." Doris's observations confirm the ideas of many educators who maintain that encouraging effective teaching is one of the most important responsibilities of instructional supervisors (Schon, 1988).

Familiarizing herself with the literature on action research (Glanz, 2003; Mills, 2002), Doris reviews the four basic steps: (a) selecting a focus for study, (b) collecting data, (c) analyzing and interpreting the data, and (d) taking action. She wonders about her classroom: "What has been successful? How do I know these strategies are successful? What needs improvement? What mistakes have I made? In what ways can I improve my instructional program?" Most important, she asks herself, "What instructional strategies that I use work best with my students in a given subject or topic?" In collaborative conversations with her assistant principal, Jim McDonnell, Doris frames her project.

She wonders whether or not the time and energy expended on cooperative learning activities are worth the effort. Although familiar with the extensive research on the subject, Doris decides to compare her fourth-period math class with her sixth-period class in terms of how cooperative learning strategies will affect student achievement and attitudes toward problem solving in mathematics. She chooses these two classes because they are somewhat equivalent in mathematical problem-solving ability. She selects a nonequivalent control group design commonly associated with ex post facto research, because the study involves the use of intact classes.

She randomly assigns "cooperative learning" as the primary instructional strategy to be used with the period 4 class, whereas the other class will work on mathematical problem solving through the traditional textbook method. After 6 weeks of implementing this plan, she administers a posttest math exam and discovers, after applying a t-test statistic, that the group exposed to cooperative learning attained significantly higher mathematical problem-solving scores than the group taught math traditionally. Doris keeps an anecdotal record throughout the research project and also administers an attitude questionnaire to ascertain how students felt about learning math using cooperative learning groups as compared to learning math in the more traditional format.

Based on her findings, Doris decides to incorporate cooperative learning procedures with all her classes. In consultation with Jim McDonnell, she develops a plan to continue assessments throughout the year. Jim asks Doris to present her findings at both grade and faculty conferences.

Doris's enthusiasm for action research is emphatic:

Employing action research engenders greater feelings of competence in solving problems and making instructional decisions. In the past I never really thought about the efficacy of my teaching methods to any great extent. The time spent in this project directly impacts on my classroom practice. I'm much more skeptical of what really works and am certainly more reflective about what I do. Action research should, I believe, be an integral part of any instructional improvement effort. No one has to convince you to change an instructional strategy. Once you gather and analyze your own data, you'll be in a position to make your own judgments about what should or should not be done. Action research empowers teachers!

Another illustration of action research as supervision is the case of the International High School (IHS), a multicultural alternative educational environment for recent arrivals to the United States, serving students with varying degrees of limited English proficiency. The school's mission is to enable each student to develop the linguistic, cognitive, and cultural skills necessary for success in high school, college, and beyond.

IHS is a learning community in which professional development is not a separate initiative but rather is built into everything that is done. The faculty and the student body are organized into six interdisciplinary teams. On each team, four teachers (math, science, English, and social studies teachers) and a support-services coordinator are jointly responsible for a heterogeneous group of about 75 9th through 12th graders. The faculty works with the same group of students for a full year, providing a complete academic program organized around themes such as "Motion," "Conflict and Resolution," or "The American Dream." Teams also provide affective and academic counseling.

The interdisciplinary teams provide an ideal infrastructure for professional development. Significant decision-making power over curriculum and even supervision is delegated to the teams. Team members engage in action research not only as an alternative to traditional supervision, but, more important, as a means to support faculty professional development and ultimately student learning.

In this second case study we find Maria Rodriguez, Bill Evans, Fred Alvaro, and Martha Cunningham (names and events are fictionalized) working together on a team. Integral to professional development at IHS is reflection. Time is structured into the workweek for planned reflection. Team members are free to brainstorm ideas on a wide variety of topics. Any team member can raise a problem or concern for group reaction. During one of these "reflective" sessions, Maria was concerned about students' test scores in writing. Other members shared her concern. Statewide examinations in writing had been mandated 2 years earlier, and the team was concerned that preliminary data indicated students were significantly deficient in this area, especially because little attention had been paid to writing under the former administration. Team members met over the summer to decide on a curriculum plan for teaching writing, eschewing prepackaged writing programs all too common in other schools in the city. After much research and in consultation with a prominent local university, the team decided to implement a rather well-known writing program sponsored by the university, although with significant modifications. Infusing writing in all content areas together with individual and small-group "writing consults," the team set out to make writing a priority in the fall semester. The team decided to field-test the new program with a randomly selected group of students in 10th grade and identified a comparable group of 10th graders not in the program.

Eric Nadelstern, the principal at the time, supporting the team, provided targeted professional development and encouraged action research strategies to track program success. He encouraged teams to use action research to demonstrate the impact of teaching on student writing achievement. As part of the program, students kept detailed writing portfolios that contained writing samples over time illustrating writing maturity. Writing assessments were continuously administered. Detailed monitoring of student progress along with constructive feedback were hallmarks of the program. After the administration of the statewide writing examination in May of that academic year, team members met to assess the impact of the program on student achievement and student writing motivation and to assess the effectiveness of the teaching strategies employed by the teachers.

The following chart summarizes their findings:

Instrument	Standard	Percentage Meeting	Conclusion
Standardized writing achievement test	50% above 50th percentile	65% above 50th percentile (25% improvement over previous year); only 35% of girls scored above norm	Expectation met; examine achievement of girls (interviews, etc.)
Writing portfolios	At least 50% scoring "acceptable" on portfolio rubric	55% scored "acceptable," but only 15% of girls did so	Expectation met overall, but examine portfolios achievement for girls
Monthly teacher-made exams	At least 50% scoring "acceptable" on writing rubric for idea development, sentence structure, and grammar	80% scored "acceptable," but significantly less for girls	Expectation met overall, but examine achievement for girls
Student surveys	At least 80% registering satisfaction with new approach to writing	70% approval rating, but only 10% for girls	Expectation not met; further study needed

Team members analyzed the data and conducted a comparative analysis with the control group. The team shared their findings with other teams and charted a course to expand the program and address the reasons why girls did not score as well as boys.

Eric Nadelstern encouraged Maria, Bill, Fred, and Martha to reflect on the process of using action research to monitor student writing progress but also to consider how such research strategies provide evidence of the impact of their teaching on student achievement. During one brainstorming session, the dialogue went something like this:

Fred:	I felt kind of empowered using alternate means of assessment to measure student writing progress. Not relying on the standardized test alone was refreshing, even though in this case the state exams reflected our qualitative and quantitative findings.
Martha:	I know what you mean. Using research strategies to track student progress helped me greatly to adjust my teaching approaches in the classroom. For instance, after monitoring their progress, I realized what worked and didn't work, and so I made changes.
Bill :	Well, that may be true, but it appears we weren't sensitive or attuned to the needs of girls. Having these data alerts us to something we may not have picked up as readily or quickly.
Martha:	You're right, Bill. I guess we first have to analyze the data more closely and perhaps collect some more information through focus groups or one-on-one interviews with some of the girls. Then we'll have to differentiate instruction to accommodate their needs, and do some more action research to ascertain any improvements. [Bill nods in affirmation, as do the others.]
Maria:	For me, this action research project provided structure to make sure I, I mean, we reflected as we proceeded. I'm not sure I would have done so myself.
Fred:	Yeah, we acted as a team . . . participating to solve a common problem.
Martha:	Also important is the fact that we were always conscious of the relationship between our teaching practices and the impact they would have on student achievement.
Eric Nadelstern [to himself]:	No need to formally observe these teachers . . . action research provided the means to encourage reflection in order to promote instructional improvement and student learning.

Suggestions for Principals

Supervision based on collaboration, participative decision making, and reflective practice is the hallmark of a viable school improvement program designed to promote teaching and learning. Action research has gradually emerged as an important form of instructional supervision in order to engage teachers in reflective practice about their teaching and as a means to examine factors that aim to promote student achievement. Practical guidelines for implementing action research as instructional improvement are now provided for you.

> "The new professional development must be different and much more powerful, and it will involve solving problems and collaborating at levels that we have never even contemplated."
>
> —Anthony Alvarado

Focus on Instructional Supervision

You are very good at compiling reports, engaging with parents, and writing proposals. Although these activities are *important,* remember to attend to *urgent* concerns. Attention to your role as instructional leader is paramount to positively affect teaching and learning. Engage teachers in instructional dialogue and meaningful supervision (not evaluation). Get out of your office into the classrooms, and save the report writing for down times and after school. Strive to encourage good pedagogy and teaching. Faculty and grade meetings should focus almost exclusively on instructional issues. Avoid quick-fix approaches that presumably guarantee high student achievement. No instructional panaceas exist. Certainly, as principal you feel the increased pressure to raise student achievement. You realize that your job is on the line. Take reasonable and intelligent steps to establish an instructional milieu in your school. Emphasize instruction at every turn— at grade and faculty conferences, through e-mail and memo correspondences, at parent workshops, and so on.

Acknowledge the importance of action research as an important component of an overall instructional supervision program.

Action research is a type of applied research that has emerged as a popular way to involve educators in reflective activities about their work. Action research is not merely defined as a narrow, limited practice but can utilize a range of methodologies, simple and complex, to better understand one's work and even solve specific instructional problems. Action research, properly used, can have immeasurable benefits, such as:

- Creating a systemwide mind-set for school improvement
- Developing a professional problem-solving ethos
- Enhancing decision making
- Promoting reflection and self-improvement
- Instilling a commitment to continuous instructional improvement
- Creating a more positive school climate in which teaching and learning are foremost concerns
- Empowering those who participate and promoting professional development

Gain Knowledge in Conducting Action Research

Action research is an ongoing process of reflection that involves four basic cyclical steps:

1. Selecting a Focus
   a. Know what you want to investigate
   b. Develop some initial questions
   c. Establish a plan to answer or better understand these questions

2. Collecting Data
   a. Primary
      Questionnaires
      Observations
      Interviews
      Tests
      Focus groups

   b. Secondary
      School profile sheets
      Multimedia
      Portfolios
      Records
      Other

3. Analyzing and Interpreting Data

4. Taking Action

Develop Stages for Implementation

The following stages for implementation were developed at Northern Valley Regional High School District (2000) and are paraphrased from a handout titled *Differentiated Supervision.*

The model allows the educator the chance to increase his or her scholarly background by encouraging him or her to examine and analyze pertinent documents. The educator might complete this independent study in 1 year. To complete the project, the educator will have periods designated for research and development during the year.

Before the educator begins the Action Research Project, he or she will discuss the project with his or her supervisor. . . . [The document emphasizes that consultations with supervisors should occur not in an evaluative or overseeing way, but in a facilitating and collaborative manner.]

At the end of the year, the researcher will submit a report to the supervisor. The report will highlight the project's significance, content, and conclusions, as well as pedagogically sound methods to teach the materials.

Approach

1. Identify the importance of the research, and suggest ways the project will enhance student achievement.

2. Identify the specific materials (primary and secondary sources) the teacher will research.

3. Develop a schedule.

4. Limit the project's scope. Such delimitation will promote thorough, rather than superficial, research.

5. Study and analyze all materials for the project.

6. Develop and implement a unit or program based on the project.

After visiting and observing Northern Valley High School District's implementation of this action research model, I can attest to the fact that a number of valuable research projects, all focusing on improving instruction, have resulted. Linking data gathered from action research with discussion on how best to promote achievement has been a primary emphasis. The emphasis on instructional improvement in Northern Valley has furthered the efficacy of action research as an invaluable means to promote student achievement. Further research is needed, however, to document the impact of action research on actually raising scores in different academic areas.

Make Time for Reflection

We've already discussed reflective practice as a process by which educational leaders take the time to contemplate and assess the efficacy of programs, products, and personnel in order to make judgments about the appropriateness or effectiveness of these so that improvements or refinements might be achieved. Research-oriented leaders have a vision that guides their work. As you plan and work to improve your schools, you collect and analyze data to better inform your decisions. As a research-oriented leader, you are engaged in ongoing self-study in which you assess the needs of your school, identify problem areas, and develop strategies for becoming more effective.

Instilling habits of reflection, critical inquiry, and training in reflection is not usually part of a principal preparatory program. Principals should submit their own practice to reflective scrutiny by posing some of these questions, among others:

1. What concerns me?

2. Why am I concerned?

3. Can I confirm my perceptions?

4. What mistakes have I made?

5. If I were able to do it again, what would I do differently?

6. What are my current options?

7. What evidence can I collect to confirm my feelings?

8. Who might be willing to share their ideas with me?

9. What have been my successes?

10. How might I replicate these successes?

11. How can I best promote instructional improvement and raise student achievement?

12. In what other ways might I improve my school?

Remember, reflection is the heart of professional practice.

Facilitate, Don't Push

Instructional supervision at IHS, in the second case study above, emerged naturally from the supportive school organizational structure. Dividing the faculty into teams encouraged reflection, teamwork, and collegiality. Providing teachers with staff development on action research empowers a faculty to implement research strategies on their own to solve or at least better understand practical problems. The principal at the school didn't have to mandate action research as supervision; it emerged as a community of learners was addressing a common concern. A wise principal establishes a conducive environment that encourages reflection. A principal sets the tone for a systemwide focus on student achievement and provides the professional development to support teachers with the resources or tools necessary to improve instruction. Action research as instructional improvement should be facilitated and encouraged.

Reflective Question

1. How could you use any of these approaches to action research as supervision in your school?

---

3. COLLABORATIVELY PLAN AND IMPLEMENT PROFESSIONAL DEVELOPMENT

What is the relationship between supervision and professional development? Although some disagreement exists (e.g., Glanz & Neville, 1997, Issue #8), many in the field now concur that supervision reconceived as a process that is nonevaluative and integral in terms of promoting instructional dialogue about teaching and learning is congruent with professional development. In fact, professional development can be seen as a way of delivering supervision. By providing professional development workshops, principals provide opportunities for teachers to engage in instructional conversations about relevant issues affecting teaching and learning. Professional development may include, among other things, participating in sessions on teaching strategies, studying the latest theory and research on practice, receiving feedback on teaching, providing resources for practice, and coaching (peer or otherwise).

The literature on professional development is vast (Speck, 1998). Almost all schools provide some sort of professional development learning opportunity for teachers. Although professional development workshops have been offered, many individuals criticize the manner in which professional development is planned and delivered. At least potentially, professional development is undoubtedly an invaluable learning activity to support teachers and to improve student learning. However, much of professional or staff development is content weak, episodic, and at its worst irrelevant to the needs of teachers.

> *"Professional Development (PD) is not a one-shot deal. It is neither a reward for good service, a treat for your good teachers, nor a break from the everyday routine of school. We believe that effective, well-conceived PD must be the primary mechanism for the continuation of instructional development and, eventually, increased student achievement."*
>
> —Albert J. Coppola,
> Diane B. Scricca, and
> Gerard E. Connors

Principals, as instructional leaders, realize that professional development—well conceived, planned, and assessed—is vital to improving teaching and student learning. Best practice in professional development points to several components as necessary (Griffin, 1997; Lieberman, 1995).

- *Purposeful and articulated.* Goals for a professional development program must be developed, examined, critiqued, and assessed for relevance. These goals must be stated in some formal way so that all educators concerned with the professional development program are clear about its intent and purpose.

- *Participatory and collaborative.* Too often, professional development is top driven, even at times by administrative fiat. Such programs are ineffective because teachers, for whom professional development provides the greatest benefit, should be actively involved in its design, implementation, and assessment. Best practice in professional development requires wide participation by all stakeholders.

- *Knowledge based.* Professional development must be based on the most relevant and current research in the field. Also, teachers will not value professional development unless it contains, in the words of one teacher, "some substance . . . something I can take back to the classroom."

- *Focused on student learning.* According to Speck (1998), "Educators must never forget that the objective of professional development is to increase student learning" (p. 156). Principals and committees responsible for planning professional development programs should consider first and foremost the teacher behaviors or activities that most directly affect student learning and then "work backward to pinpoint the knowledge, skills, and attitudes educators must have" (p. 157).

- *Ongoing.* Too much professional development is of the "one-shot" variety. A leader delivers a workshop, for instance, and then leaves without any follow-up. Such efforts have marginal value at best. Professional development opportunities must be made on a continuous basis so that ideas and practices are sustained. Professional development cannot affect classroom practice in a significant way unless workshops and programs are continually offered.

- *Developmental.* Professional development must be not only ongoing but developmental; that is, it must build gradually on teacher knowledge and skills in a given area or topic.

- *Analytical and reflective.* Professional development opportunities must promote instructional dialogue and thinking about teaching practice and purposefully address ways of helping students achieve more. Also, professional development must be continuously assessed in terms of its relevance and value to teachers.

Reflective Question

1. How would you plan, implement, and assess a professional development program for your school? Be specific.

---

4. PROMOTE INSTRUCTION THROUGH PCOWBIRDS

You can incorporate best practice by following a mnemonic known as PCOWBIRDS (a strategy I learned from Dr. Thomas Monterro in workshops leading to my certification as a principal in New York City), which includes information useful in addressing and promoting instructional matters.

As a competent instructional leader, you should attend to *PCOWBIRDS!*

P = Plans: Planning is integral to instructional success, and the principal as an educational leader should help a teacher develop appropriate and meaningful instructional activities and learning experiences. Checking plans, offering suggestions, coplanning, reviewing procedures, and framing thought-provoking questions, among other important activities, are essential. Supervision, then, involves assisting teachers to better plan their lessons and units of instruction.

C = Conferences: Conferencing with teachers, formally and informally, in order to share ideas and develop alternate instructional strategies is an essential supervisory responsibility. Meeting and talking with teachers throughout the day and school year on instructional matters is essential. Your focus as an instructional leader must be on teaching and learning. Sharing insights, reviewing recent research (Marzano, Pickering, & Pollock, 2001), and engaging in reflective practice are very important. Formal and informal conferencing must be continuous and should involve teachers in the planning and agenda of conferences. The key to establishing a grade or school culture that fosters instructional dialogue for the purpose of improving teaching and learning is to consider such activity your number-one priority and, thus, to devote time and energy to ensuring and nurturing it.

O = Observations: An educational leader should offer her or his expertise by both formally and informally observing classroom interaction. A skilled principal who utilizes various observation systems (e.g., Acheson & Gall, 1997; Glickman et al., 2005; Sullivan & Glanz, 2005) can facilitate instructional improvement by documenting classroom interaction so that a teacher might reflect upon and react to what has been observed. Providing teachers with evidence of classroom interaction is fundamental to begin helping them understand what they are doing or not doing to promote student learning. Observations play a key role in supervision. As Yogi Berra once quipped, "You can observe a lot by watching."

W = Workshops: Principals as educational leaders should conduct or organize various workshops for teachers on relevant instructional topics such as cooperative learning, alternative teaching strategies, and multiple intelligences. Sometimes principals will feel comfortable in conducting a workshop. Principals are not expected, of course, to be conversant in all areas. Sometimes they may ask an outside consultant or expert in a particular field to conduct a workshop on a topic of interest to teachers or even ask one of the more experienced teachers to do so. The bottom line here is that you, as principal, realize the importance of instruction as the main focus of your work. Realizing the importance of instruction, you plan and coordinate varied and continuous workshops for teachers. These workshops may be conducted as a part of professional development days designated by the school or district, as part of a grade or faculty conference, or as an activity planned for after or before school or even during the summer.

B = Bulletins: Bulletins, journals, reports, and newsletters can be disseminated to interested faculty. One of my teachers became interested in cooperative learning after attending a reading conference. I sustained her interest by placing several articles about cooperative learning in her mailbox. Principals are conversant with the literature of various fields and subscribe to various journals including *Educational Leadership, Kappan, Journal of Curriculum and Supervision, Elementary School Journal, Instructor, Teaching K–12, Journal of Learning Disabilities,* and so forth. Principals are always on the alert for relevant articles, bulletins, and publications that encourage and support instructional improvement.

I = Intervisitations: Teachers rarely have the opportunity to visit and observe colleagues. A principal can facilitate intervisitations by rearranging the schedule so that teachers might observe one another and then share common instructional strategies or discuss common problems. Intervisitations, to be effective, must be voluntary and nonjudgmental. Shared dialogue about instructional practices goes a long way toward promoting instructional improvement.

R = Resources: Principals should make available for teachers a variety of instructional materials and technologies to enhance instructional improvement. Purchasing textbooks, trade books, computers, LCD projectors, and other relevant resources is important to support an instructional program.

D = Demonstration lessons: A principal presumably is a teacher of teachers. A principal is not necessarily the foremost teacher in a school, but he or she should feel comfortable in providing "demo" lessons for teachers when appropriate. Providing such lessons enhances supervisory credibility among teachers and provides instructional support.

Parenthetically, I once noticed during a formal observation that the teacher was not using wait time effectively. He posed good questions but waited only about 2 seconds before calling on someone. I suggested that he watch me teach a lesson and notice how long I wait after posing a question before calling on a pupil. These observations were the basis for a follow-up conference at which we discussed the research on "wait time" and the advantages of waiting before calling on a pupil. As the saying goes, "a picture is worth a thousand words." Having this particular teacher watch me demonstrate effective use of "wait time" was more valuable than if I had merely told him what to do. Competent supervisors not only "suggest" how to do something, they also must "demonstrate" how it should be done.

S = Staff development: Principals can aid instructional improvement by providing staff development that is "purposeful and articulated," "participatory and collaborative," "knowledge-based," "ongoing," "developmental," and "analytic and reflective" (Griffin, 1997). Although I addressed workshops above, staff development means a series of collaboratively planned and implemented workshops on a single topic or varied topics over time. Understanding the relationship between staff development and instructional improvement is critical. Teachers need continued and sustained instructional support. A good principal will plan for such meaningful staff or professional development.

So as you strive to promote instructional improvement, keep in mind PCOWBIRDS.

Reflective Question

1. How might PCOWBIRDS serve as a useful mnemonic to help you develop and maintain an instructional emphasis in your work?

CONCLUSION

Providing instructional leadership by focusing on best practices in supervision and professional development is your prime responsibility. Unfortunately, much supervisory practice and many professional development activities are not very useful for teachers. You can contribute greatly to meaningful supervision and professional development by engaging in these leadership behaviors:

- In word and deed, place emphasis on improving teaching and promoting learning.
- Involve teachers in planning, implementing, and assessing supervision and professional development.

- Utilize experts in supervision and professional development as consultants.
- Provide options or alternatives to traditional practices of supervision and professional development.
- Draw links between supervision and professional development and student achievement.

CHAPTER FIVE

Promoting Student Achievement for All

"In a high-stakes context, school leaders must search for ways to create a culture of high expectations and support for all students and a set of norms around teacher growth that enables teachers to teach all students well."

—Linda Lambert

A major premise of this book is that effective principals make a difference in student learning. Engaging in best teaching, curriculum, and supervision practices, principals aim to promote student achievement. In fact, as a principal you cannot be considered successful unless student achievement levels increase. Student achievement will not increase by your attending only to cultural, ethical, school-community, collaborative, operational, and strategic leadership. You can develop partnerships with the community or develop the most detailed and well-written strategic plan, but unless they help lead to raising student achievement, their value is marginal. Each of these aforementioned kinds of leadership is certainly essential, but unless you emphasize your role as an instructional leader you will not be successful. Effective principals understand the synchronous relationship among these types of leadership (which, by the way, comprise this book series). They all are necessary to make instructional leadership possible, but again, without focusing on instruction as the main enterprise most directly linked to student achievement, your leadership will be compromised.

This chapter succinctly reviews extant research that confirms the link between effective principals and student achievement. Relying on the groundbreaking work of Cotton (2003), I will review 26 research-based principal behaviors and characteristics of principals as instructional leaders that are positively related to student achievement. Effective principals do not operate in isolation of others; they encourage cooperation and collaboration in most, if not all, of the following behaviors.

26 BEST PRACTICE LEADERSHIP PRINCIPAL BEHAVIORS

Effective principals:

> "A key difference between highly effective and less effective principals is that the former are actively involved in the curricular and instructional life of their schools."
>
> —Kathleen Cotton

- Establish a safe and orderly school environment by communicating high expectations for student behavior (you can't have high student achievement in a chaotic environment in which student misbehavior is tolerated)
- Articulate a vision that includes clear goals for student learning
- Communicate high expectations for student achievement (you also must encourage teachers to demonstrate their belief that all students can achieve)
- Persevere despite setbacks (student achievement doesn't occur linearly; sometimes, actually most often, students may falter academically until a breakthrough occurs; good principals understand this fact and don't panic)

- Maintain a high profile (effective principals are always available to support teachers instructionally)
- Support positive school climate by encouraging and nurturing a caring school
- Communicate the importance of instructional excellence
- Attend to the personal and emotional needs of students and teachers
- Reach out to parents and community for assistance with both instruction and school governance
- Demonstrate their commitment to instructional excellence through symbolic leadership (e.g., one principal I know vowed to shave his head if student achievement in reading rose more than one grade level schoolwide. I am not of course recommending you follow suit, but do realize the importance of symbolic actions)
- Encourage participative decision making with teachers and staff regarding instructional issues
- Support a cooperative schoolwide learning environment
- Actively and continuously engage in instructional matters and decisions
- Actively and continuously engage others in instructional matters and decisions
- Establish a norm of continuous improvement by continually pushing for improvement in student performance
- Engage faculty in instructional and curricular matters at every turn
- Visit classrooms frequently, observing and providing feedback continuously (Downey et al., 2004)
- Respect teacher autonomy and do not excessively intrude
- Support teacher risk taking involving trying out innovative instructional strategies
- Secure ample instructional resources (personnel or otherwise) to implement professional development
- Avoid administrative intrusions such as loudspeaker announcements
- Monitor student academic progress systematically
- Interpret performance data and use such data to make instructional improvements
- Acknowledge the accomplishments of faculty in terms of their hard work to improve student performance and to recognize students for their individual achievements

- "Walk the talk" (i.e., they don't just talk about improving instruction, they take specific actions that demonstrate their commitment to instruction)
- Avoid bureaucratic or autocratic practices that stifle teacher autonomy

All of these principal behaviors are research based and have been found to be positively related to student achievement (Cotton, 2003). Cotton concludes her extensive review of the literature on principal behaviors and student achievement by stating:

Can the importance of the principal's role in fostering student achievement be overstated? The principal does not affect student performance single-handedly, of course, or even directly. Yet the evidence clearly shows that . . . principals do have a profound and positive influence on student learning. The converse is also true: High-achieving schools whose principals do not lead in these ways are difficult to find. So difficult, in fact, that veteran researcher Lawrence Lezotte has gone so far as to say, "If you know of an effective school without an effective principal, call me collect." (p. 74)

Reflective Question

1. Taking each of the 26 points mentioned above, explain what you would do to practically and specifically address each behavior or characteristic.

Conclusion

Making the Time for
Instructional Leadership

"**P**roviding instructional leadership? Who has the time?" asks a principal in an inner-city school in Los Angeles. "Certainly, we've learned about curriculum development and clinical supervision in graduate courses, but who has much time to really implement them when you're on the job?" complains another principal in a suburban school in Westchester, New York. "Constant emergencies, student misbehavior, and being drained from lunch duties prevent me from working with teachers on the improvement of instruction," complains another principal. Anyone who has worked as a principal in a fairly large school setting realizes that it's difficult to devote much time to instructional improvement.

How, then, can a principal find the time to engage in instructional leadership? The following are some suggestions, drawn in part from the work of Michael Fullan and Andy Hargreaves (1996).

Locate, listen to, and articulate your inner voice. To quote Fullan and Hargreaves (1996):

> Often, when we say we have no time for something, it's an evasion. What we mean is we have more immediate or convenient things to do with that time. Of course, bulletin boards and visual aids are important. But doing them doesn't make you feel personally uncomfortable. It isn't disquieting. It isn't a personal challenge. Listening to our inner voice is. It

requires not just time, but courage and commitment too. (pp. 65–66)

Believe that you can make a difference. The importance of working to promote instructional improvement has been stressed. Commit to continuous improvement and perpetual learning as a foremost goal. Principals must demonstrate the "intestinal fortitude," if you will, to "push themselves to create the professional learning environments they want" (Fullan & Hargreaves, 1996, p. 82). More than that, principals must believe that they can make a difference (Denham & Michael, 1981).

Principals who are comfortable with providing instructional support to teachers are likely to have been good teachers themselves. Moreover, they have the knowledge and skills to design and implement programs and activities that provide instructional growth opportunities for teachers. Such principals will find the time for instructional leadership because they value it and truly believe that it makes a difference in teacher development and student achievement. The mark of a good school is one in which instructional leadership is primary. Schools must consciously seek principals who are instructional leaders.

Resource A

Realities of Instructional
Leadership: In-Basket Simulations

T his section highlights some of the realities of instructional leadership using an approach called "In-Basket
Simulations." It is a study technique derived from an approach
used when I studied for licensure as a principal in New York City.
The approach was developed by the Institute for Research and
Professional Development (http://www.nycenet.edu/opm/opm/
profservices/rfp1b723.html). Scenarios that you as a principal
might encounter are presented for your reaction. For instance, "a
letter from an irate parent complaining that her child is intention-
ally being ignored during instruction in class by the teacher is
sent to your attention. What would you do?" Challenging you to
confront real-life phenomena under controlled conditions, these
simulated in-basket items, some of which are culled from workshops I attended while seeking initial principal certification, will
prompt critical inquiry.

Here are suggestions to guide you as you complete these
in-basket exercises:

1. Think and respond as if you are a principal, not a teacher
   or, perhaps, an assistant principal.

2. Place yourself mentally in each situation as if the case
   were actually happening to you.

3. Draw on your experiences and on what you've learned
   from others. Think of a principal you respect and ask yourself, "What would Mr. or Ms. X have done?"

4. Make distinctions between actions you would personally take and actions you would delegate to others.

5. Utilize resources (personnel or otherwise) to assist you.

6. Think about your response, then share it with a colleague for her or his reaction.

7. Record your response, and then a day later reread the scenario and your response. Would you still have reacted the same way?

During an interview you are asked to respond to the following scenarios (first three bullets):

• React to the following statements: *Certainly instructional improvement is necessary. Not all principals, though, are "super" teachers. Rather, a good principal knows how to select other instructional leaders. The role of the principal is to oversee their job and ensure that enough time is paid to instructional improvement.*

• What would you do to encourage teachers to trust that you are there to "help" them and not merely to "evaluate" them? (Here are some suggested solutions, offered merely to get you started: *Tell them so; show them so by not writing an evaluation that includes information gleaned during one of your "helping" sessions; help them at every opportunity; get them some extra monies/supplies to support classroom instruction.*)

• How would you forge a role for yourself as an instructional leader and not merely a manager, especially in a school in which the former principal did not focus on instruction? (Here are some suggested solutions: *Allot time for instructional involvement with faculty; conduct a demonstration lesson for them occasionally; discuss teaching and learning with them on many occasions; conduct workshops on various topics of teacher interest and bring in speakers to discuss instructional issues.*)

• The former principal was an administrator type, not an instructional leader. Your faculty are used to the traditional method of evaluation. How would you establish a culture supportive of clinical supervisory practice? Be specific. (Here are some suggested solutions: *Begin small by collaborating with a like-minded and receptive teacher or two about your ideas; field-test your ideas with them; conduct a demonstration lesson; invite a teacher or two to visit another school where the cycle works.*)

- You are a newly assigned principal in a K–5 elementary school. The superintendent has indicated that she is not pleased with the results of the instructional program being provided to children who have been held over because of their lack of progress in class work and their poor performances on standardized reading and math tests. The held-over children are placed together in the same class on the grade. The superintendent requests that you review the situation and make recommendations to her. Describe with justifications four recommendations you would submit to the superintendent for improving the instructional program for these held-over children so that they can function more effectively in the school. (Here are some suggested solutions: *Develop a needs assessment committee to analyze past practices and suggest new directions; examine curricular materials used with students, and consider more up-to-date curriculum materials; develop an instructional plan that stresses effective remediation; work out motivational strategies to excite held-over children; plan an action research study, e.g., pre- and posttests, to determine effectiveness of program.*)

- You are a principal at a local high school that has an excellent reputation for its rigorous curriculum. You receive an anonymous note in your mailbox informing you that Mr. O'Hare is teaching topics that are not part of the prescribed history curriculum and that students will not be prepared for the statewide competency exam. Assuming that the allegations are verified, describe your actions. (Here are some possible solutions or approaches: *Observe the teacher; speak with the teacher in private to ascertain reasons; explain why adherence to curriculum is important while supporting teacher's creativity to extend the curriculum, where and when appropriate; with teacher's permission, bring issue of "teaching to the curriculum" up at a faculty or grade conference for open discussion.*)

- You are assigned as a principal in a middle school in an urban area in which teachers complain that they are unable to teach their subject area because of the students' poor reading skills. Outline the steps you would take in dealing with the teachers and in improving the reading abilities of the students. Include the techniques, services, and personnel you would utilize. Discuss the curriculum development initiatives you would take. (Base your curriculum response on information in this book, but feel free to vary your responses in terms of your knowledge of dealing with reading difficulties; be sure to include discussing the problem with an expert in the field.)

- Explain how you would use your schoolwide assessment system to improve instruction in general. More specifically, let's say that your data indicate that students are ill prepared to use technology in meaningful, educational ways. What would you do to ensure that all students are "technologically" competent? (You're on your own on this one).

- You are passionate about inclusive practice and want to increase the number of inclusion classes in your school. Some vocal parents inform you that they will resist such an increase, because they don't want their children's education jeopardized by having special education students in the same classroom as their children. Explain the steps you might take to develop more meaningful inclusive practices in your school and describe how you would ensure high achievement for all students in your school in general. (You're on your own on this one, too.)

Don't forget to share responses with colleagues, because good discussion about these instructional issues will clarify your thoughts, expose you to viewpoints different from your own, and raise even more questions for consideration. Again, there are few principal tasks more important than instructional leadership, the theme of this book.

Resource B

Assessing Your Role as Instructional Leader

C harlotte Danielson, in a 1996 work titled *Enhancing Professional Practice: A Framework for Teaching*, published by the Association for Supervision and Curriculum Development, developed a framework or model for understanding teaching based on current research in the field. She identified "components" clustered into four domains of teaching responsibility: planning and preparation, classroom environment, instruction, and professional responsibilities. I adapted and developed the questionnaire below based on her framework. Please take the survey now, because it will *serve as an important reflective tool to judge what you consider as instructionally important.* Please note that your responses are private. Therefore, your honest responses to the various items below will best assist you in becoming an *even better instructional leader.*

SA = Strongly Agree ("For the most part, yes.")

A = Agree ("Yes, but . . .")

D = Disagree ("No, but . . .")

SD = Strongly Disagree ("For the most part, no.")

Planning and Preparation

SA   A   D   SD   1. Teachers should be offered guidance in planning and preparing for instruction, and I feel comfortable in doing so.

SA   A   D   SD   2. Good teachers should display solid content knowledge and make connections between the parts of their discipline or with other disciplines.

SA   A   D   SD   3. Good teachers should consider the importance of prerequisite knowledge when introducing new topics.

SA   A   D   SD   4. Good teachers actively build on students' prior knowledge and seek causes for students' misunderstanding.

SA   A   D   SD   5. Good teachers are content knowledgeable but may need additional assistance with pedagogical strategies and techniques, and I feel comfortable providing such assistance.

SA   A   D   SD   6. I am familiar with pedagogical strategies and continually search for best practices to share with my teachers.

SA   A   D   SD   7. Good teachers know much about the developmental needs of their students.

SA   A   D   SD   8. Principals are familiar with learning styles and multiple intelligences theories and can help teachers apply them to instructional practice.

SA   A   D   SD   9. I do not fully recognize the value of understanding teachers' skills and knowledge as a basis for their teaching.

SA   A   D   SD   10. Goal setting is critical to teacher success in planning and preparing, and the principal should offer to collaborate with teachers in this area.

SA   A   D   SD   11. I am familiar with curricular and teaching resources to assist teachers.

SA   A   D   SD   12. I know I can help teachers develop appropriate learning activities suitable for students.

SA   A   D   SD   13. I can help teachers plan for a variety of meaningful learning activities matched to school, district, and state instructional goals.

SA   A   D   SD   14. I would encourage teachers to use varied instructional grouping.

SA   A   D   SD   15. I can assist teachers in developing a systematic plan for assessment of student learning.

SA   A   D   SD   16. I can provide professional development for teachers in planning and preparation.

The Classroom Environment

SA   A   D   SD   1. I realize the importance of classroom management and discipline.

SA   A   D   SD   2. I expect that teacher interactions with students are generally friendly and demonstrate warmth and caring.

SA   A   D   SD   3. I expect teachers to develop a system of discipline without my assistance.

SA   A   D   SD   4. I will play an active role in monitoring grade and school discipline plans.

SA   A   D   SD   5. I support the classroom teachers in matters of discipline.

SA   A   D   SD   6. I always communicate high expectations to all my teachers that they are the critical element in the classroom.

SA   A   D   SD   7. I expect teachers to have a well-established and well-defined system of rules and procedures.

SA   A   D   SD   8. I expect that teachers are alert to student behavior at all times.

SA   A   D   SD   9. I can provide professional development to teachers on classroom management.

SA   A   D   SD   10. As a teacher, I was a competent classroom manager.

Instruction

SA   A   D   SD   1. I expect that teachers' directions to students will be clear and not confusing.

SA   A   D   SD   2. My directives to teachers about instruction are clear.

SA   A   D   SD   3. My spoken language as a teacher was clear and appropriate according to the grade level of my students.

SA   A   D   SD   4. I believe that teacher questioning techniques are among the most critical skills needed to promote pupil learning, and I feel comfortable helping teachers frame good questions.

SA   A   D   SD   5. Teacher questions must be of uniformly high quality.

SA   A   D   SD   6. From my experience, teachers mostly lecture (talk) to students without enough student participation.

SA A D SD   7. I encourage teachers to encourage students to participate and prefer for students to take an active role in learning.

SA A D SD   8. I can provide a workshop for teachers on giving assignments that are appropriate to students and that engage students mentally.

SA A D SD   9. I don't know how to group students appropriately for instruction.

SA A D SD   10. I am very familiar with grouping strategies to promote instruction.

SA A D SD   11. I can advise teachers on how best to select appropriate and effective instructional materials and resources.

SA A D SD   12. My demo lessons to teachers are highly coherent, and my pacing is consistent and appropriate.

SA A D SD   13. I rarely provide appropriate feedback to my teachers.

SA A D SD   14. Feedback to my teachers is consistent, appropriate, and of high quality.

SA A D SD   15. I expect my teachers to rely heavily on the teacher's manual for instruction.

SA A D SD   16. I consistently encourage teachers to seek my advice on teaching and learning matters.

SA A D SD   17. I encourage teachers to use wait time effectively.

SA   A   D   SD   18. I feel competent enough to give a workshop to teachers on effective use of wait time.

SA   A   D   SD   19. I consider myself an instructional leader.

SA   A   D   SD   20. Teachers perceive me as an instructional leader.

Professional Responsibilities

SA   A   D   SD   1. I have difficulty assessing the effectiveness of teachers.

SA   A   D   SD   2. I can accurately assess how well I am doing as an instructional leader.

SA   A   D   SD   3. I really don't know how to improve teaching skills.

SA   A   D   SD   4. I am aware of what I need to do in order to become an effective instructional leader.

SA   A   D   SD   5. I rarely encourage parents to become involved in instructional matters.

SA   A   D   SD   6. I actively and consistently engage parents to visit classrooms.

SA   A   D   SD   7. I feel comfortable giving workshops to parents on curricular and instructional matters.

SA   A   D   SD   8. I have difficulty relating to my colleagues in a cordial and professional manner.

SA   A   D   SD   9. I collaborate with my colleagues in a cordial and professional manner.

SA   A   D   SD   10. I avoid becoming involved in school and district projects.

SA   A   D   SD   11. I rarely encourage teachers to engage in professional development activities.

SA   A   D   SD   12. I seek out opportunities for professional development to enhance my pedagogical skills.

SA   A   D   SD   13. I am rarely alert to teachers' instructional needs.

SA   A   D   SD   14. I serve teachers.

SA   A   D   SD   15. I am an advocate for students' rights.

SA   A   D   SD   16. I am an advocate for teachers' rights.

SA   A   D   SD   17. I rarely encourage teachers to serve on a school-based committee.

SA   A   D   SD   18. I enjoy working with teachers collaboratively on instructional matters.

Analyze your responses:

Note that the items above draw from research that highlights good educational practice. Review your responses and circle responses that concern you. For instance, if you circled *Strongly Agree* for "I am rarely alert to teachers' instructional needs," ask yourself, "Why is this a problem?" "How can I remedy the situation?" and "What additional resources or assistance might I need?" If you agree, share and compare responses with another educator. The dialogue that will ensue will serve as a helpful vehicle to move toward more effective practice.

In summary, review your responses for each of the four domains as noted below:

Domain 1: Planning and Preparation. This domain demonstrates your comfort level in working with teachers on content and pedagogical knowledge, knowledge of students and resources, ability to select instructional goals, and the degree to which you help teachers assess learning.

SA   A   D   SD   1. My ability to work with teachers on planning and preparation is satisfactory.

Domain 2: The Classroom Environment. This domain assesses the degree to which you encourage and create an environment of respect and caring and establish a culture for learning related to many aspects of classroom environment.

SA   A   D   SD   1. I am satisfied that my ability to work with teachers on the classroom environment is satisfactory.

Domain 3: Instruction. This domain assesses the ability to work with teachers to communicate with clarity, use questioning and discussion techniques, engage students in learning, provide feedback to students, and demonstrate flexibility and responsiveness to students' instructional needs.

SA   A   D   SD   1. I am satisfied that my knowledge and skills of instruction are satisfactory.

Domain 4: Professional Responsibilities. This domain assesses the degree to which you encourage teachers to reflect on teaching, maintain accurate records, communicate with parents, contribute to the school and district, grow and develop professionally, and show professionalism.

SA   A   D   SD   1. I am satisfied that I am professionally responsible.

Resource C

An Annotated Bibliography of Best Resources

The literature on the principalship and related areas is extensive. The following list is not meant to serve as a comprehensive resource by any means. The selected titles I have annotated are few but, in my opinion, are among the most useful references on the subject. Rather than "impress" you with a more extensive list, I have selected these outstanding works related specifically to instructional leadership that will supplement my book quite well. I may have missed, of course, many other important works. Nevertheless, this list is a good start. I've also included some topics of related interest. Don't forget that life is a long journey of continuous learning. Continue to hone your skills by reading good books and journal articles on instructional leadership. No one is ever perfect, and everyone can learn something new by keeping current with the literature in the field. Share your readings and reactions with a colleague.

Instructional Leadership

Blase, J., & Blase, J. (2004). *Handbook of instructional leadership: How successful principals promote teaching and learning.* Thousand Oaks, CA: Corwin.

One of the most comprehensive treatments of instructional leadership, this book should serve as the bible for principal instructional leadership. The second edition expands the scope of the topic by explicating in concrete ways how instructional leaders inspire their staff to develop professional learning communities. This book serves as both a theoretical exposition and a practical guide to maximizing teaching and learning.

Glickman, C. D. (2002). *Leadership for learning: How to help teachers succeed.* Alexandria, VA: Association for Supervision and Curriculum Development.

Practical guidance to help teachers improve classroom teaching and learning. Easy to use and reader friendly.

McEwan, E. K. (2003). *Seven steps to effective instructional leadership* (2nd ed.). Thousand Oaks, CA: Corwin.

Another practical, research- and standards-based, hands-on guide to becoming an effective instructional leader. Packed with concrete suggestions, this book is a must-read.

Pajak, E. (2000). *Approaches to clinical supervision: Alternatives for improving instruction* (2nd ed.). Norwood, MA: Christopher-Gordon.

An excellent review of models of supervision.

Zepeda, S. J. (2003). *The principal as instructional leader: A handbook for supervisors.* Larchmont, NY: Eye on Education.

Very helpful workbook accompanied by a CD that contains electronic versions of many of the forms provided throughout this useful work.

Books to Recommend for Teachers

Abbey, O. F., Jr. (2003). *A practical guide for new teachers: Getting started, surviving, and succeeding.* Norwood, MA: Christopher-Gordon.

A short, practical guide for new teachers that includes advice from how to obtain a teaching position to what life in school is like and how to survive in the classroom.

Armstrong, T. (1998). *How to awaken genius in the classroom.* Alexandria, VA: Association for Supervision and Curriculum Development.

Some may consider this book "far-out," but I think its thesis is true and a must-read—a really short book.

Ayers, W. (1993). *To teach: The journey of a teacher.* New York: Teachers College Press.

Inspiring introduction to teaching.

Canter, L. (1992). *Assertive discipline.* Santa Monica, CA: Lee Canter and Associates.

The very best book on corrective discipline out there! Learn and practice the difference among the three response styles. Although controversial (some hate the system, others swear by it), I'm in the latter camp. Recommend it! A life saver!!

Delpit, L. (1988). *Other people's children: Cultural conflict in the classroom.* New York: New Press.

One of the most widely read books; a must-read for those who care for "others' children."

Gill, V. (2001). *The eleven commandments of good teaching: Creating classrooms where teachers can teach and students can learn* (2nd ed.). Thousand Oaks, CA: Corwin.

Really concise and useful. Don't let the catchy title fool you; this book is excellent. Full of tactics and strategies, this resource is written by a veteran teacher who has practical and wise advice.

Ginott, H. G. (1972). *Between teacher and child.* New York: Macmillan.

If I could recommend only one book, this would be it! Sensitive, insightful, and practical, this work is a classic in the field. An "oldie but goodie."

Nieto, S. (1996). *Affirming diversity: The sociopolitical context of multicultural education.* New York: Longman.

Also a classic on diversity.

Tatum, D. B. (1997). *Why are all the black kids sitting together in the cafeteria?* New York: Basic Books.

Phenomenal, life changing, and practical.

Wong, H. K., & Wong, R. T. (1998). *How to be an effective teacher: The first days of school.* Mountain View, CA: Harry K. Wong.

Wong is an inspirational speaker, and his national bestseller is a must-read not only for every beginning teacher but even for experienced teachers, to remind them of the basics and to inspire them.

Instructional Strategies

Gregory, G. H., & Chapman, C. (2002). *Differentiated instructional strategies: One size doesn't fit all.* Thousand Oaks, CA: Corwin.

Practical strategies and techniques.

Harmin, M. (1994). *Inspiring active learning: A handbook for teachers.* Alexandria, VA: Association for Supervision and Curriculum Development.

If I could recommend only one book for you to read on practical strategies to promote learning, then this book would be the one! Don't miss it. See http://www.inspiringonline.com/History.html.

Saphier, J., & Gower, R. (1997). *The skillful teacher* (5th ed.). Acton, MA: Research for Better Teaching.

Classic that combines theory and practice really well. A popular college text, but very reader friendly.

Tileston, D. W. (2004). *What every teacher should know about . . .* Thousand Oaks, CA: Corwin.

This 10-book series inspired this book and series on the principalship. Principals who are a bit insecure about instructional leadership or who want to brush up on a host of topics related to teaching and learning should read this superb series. The 10 topics included are diverse learners; student motivation; learning, memory, and the brain; instructional planning; effective teaching strategies; classroom management and discipline; student assessment; special learners; media and technology; and the profession and politics of teaching.

Tomlinson, C. A. (2001). *How to differentiate instruction in mixed-ability classrooms* (2nd ed.). Alexandria, VA: Association for Supervision and Curriculum Development.

Provides easy-to-read and useful practical strategies for how teachers can navigate a diverse classroom. If you want to learn how to teach students of different abilities at the same time, read this book—great case studies of classrooms at all levels in which instruction is differentiated successfully.

Journals and Newspapers

The Clearing House
Education Week
The Educational Forum
Educational Leadership
Equity & Excellence in Education
Harvard Educational Review
Kappan

Learning & Leading with Technology
NASSP Bulletin
Phi Delta Kappa Fastbacks
Principal
Teachers College Record

Personal Growth

Glanz, J. (2000). *Relax for success: An educator's guide to stress management.* Norwood, MA: Christopher-Gordon.

My suggestions for a successful life and career.

Whitaker, T., & Winkle, J. (2001). *Feeling great: The educator's guide for eating better, exercising smarter, and feeling your best.* Larchmont, NY: Eye on Education.

Wonderful reference work.

Research on Instruction and Teaching

Danielson, C. (1996). *Enhancing professional practice: A framework for teaching.* Alexandria, VA: Association for Supervision and Curriculum Development.

Author has developed a framework or model for understanding teaching based on current research in the field.

Marzano, R. J., Pickering, D. J., & Pollock, J. E. (2001). *Classroom instruction that works: Research-based strategies for increasing student achievement.* Alexandria, VA: Association for Supervision and Curriculum Development.

Authors examine decades of research in education to come up with nine teaching strategies that have positive effects on student learning—one of the books that is a must-read.

Stronge, J. H. (2002). *Qualities of effective teachers.* Alexandria, VA: Association for Supervision and Curriculum Development.

The most recent and also one of the best summaries of current research on teacher effectiveness.

Research on Principals and Student Achievement

Cotton, K. (2003). *Principals and student achievement: What research says.* Alexandria, VA: Association for Supervision and Curriculum Development.

The author has done an admirable job of synthesizing the vast literature on principals' characteristics and student achievement. Excellent section of annotated references that reviews extant research on principals and the impact on student achievement.

Web Sites

http://www.google.com

Great advice: search Google by typing in *principals*—now, spend the day exploring. Google is most accessible, easy to use, and current.

http://www.corwinpress.com

Refer to the veritable storehouse of wisdom contained in other Corwin publications. Visit the site to request a catalog or call 800-818-7243.

http://www.nassp.org/

National Association of Secondary School Principals—a must resource.

http://edstandards.org/Standards.html

Great site to help principals help teachers understand the relation of national and state standards to their own town and city standards.

http://www.glef.org/php/people.php?id=C501641

This site highlights the work of Grant Wiggins, assessment guru. Although this book has not addressed assessment in detail, instructional leaders should work with teachers on establishing a systematic, sensible approach to assessment. Collecting data in order to ultimately improve the instructional program is imperative.

References

Acheson, K. A., & Gall, M. D. (1997). *Techniques in the clinical supervision of teachers.* New York: Longman.

Amrein, A. L., & Berliner, D. C. (2003). The effects of high-stakes testing on student motivation and learning. *Educational Leadership, 60,* 32–38.

Anyon, J. (1997). *Ghetto schooling: A political economy of urban educational reform.* New York: Teachers College Press.

Beach, D. M. (2000). *Supervisory leadership: Focus on instruction.* Boston: Allyn & Bacon.

Beach, D. M., & Reinhartz, J. (2000). *Supervisory leadership: Focus on instruction.* Boston: Allyn & Bacon.

Beck, L. G., & Murphy, J. (1993). *Understanding the principalship: Metaphorical themes, 1920s–1990s.* New York: Teachers College Press.

Blase, J., & Blase, J. (2004). *Handbook of instructional leadership: How successful principals promote teaching and learning.* Thousand Oaks, CA: Corwin.

Bransford, J. D., Brown, A. L., & Cocking, R. R. (Eds.). (1999). *How people learn: Brain, mind, experience, and school.* Washington, DC: National Academy Press.

Chomsky, N. (2002). *Chomsky offers advice to teachers on the use of science.* Retrieved February 16, 2005, from http://www.justresponse.net/chomsky_offers_advice.html

Coppola, A. J., Scricca, D. B., & Connors, G. E. (2004). *Supportive supervision: Becoming a teacher of teachers.* Thousand Oaks, CA: Corwin.

Costa, A. L., & Garmston, R. J. (2002). *Cognitive coaching: A foundation for renaissance schools* (2nd ed.). Norwood, MA: Christopher-Gordon.

Cotton, K. (2003). *Principals and student achievement: What research says.* Alexandria, VA: Association for Supervision and Curriculum Development.

Cremin, L. (1964). *Transformation of the school: Progressivism in American education, 1876–1957.* New York: Random House.

Danielson, C. (1996). *Enhancing professional practice: A framework for teaching.* Alexandria, VA: Association for Supervision and Curriculum Development.

Denham, C., & Michael, J. (1981). Teacher sense of efficacy: An important factor in school improvement. *Elementary School Journal, 86,* 173–184.

DeRoche, E. F. (1987). *An administrator's guide for evaluating programs and personnel: An effective schools approach* (2nd ed.). Boston: Allyn & Bacon.

Dewey, J. (1899). *The school and society.* Chicago: University of Chicago Press.

Downey, C. J., Steffy, B. E., English, F. W., Frase, L. E., & Poston, W. K., Jr. (2004). *The three-minute walk-through: Changing school supervisory practice one teacher at a time.* Thousand Oaks, CA: Corwin.

Fisher, D., Frey, N., & Williams, D. (2002). Seven literacy strategies that work. *Educational Leadership, 60,* 70–73.

Foote, C. S., Vermette, P. J., & Battaglia, C. F. (2001). *Constructivist strategies: Meeting standards and engaging adolescent minds.* Larchmont, NY: Eye on Education.

Fullan, M., & Hargreaves, A. (1996). *What's worth fighting for in your school.* New York: Teachers College Press.

Ginott, H. (1993). *Teacher and child: A book for parents and teachers.* New York: Macmillan.

Glanz, J. (2003). *Action research: An educational leader's guide to school improvement.* Norwood, MA: Christopher-Gordon.

Glanz, J. (2004a). *The assistant principal's handbook: Strategies for success.* Thousand Oaks, CA: Corwin.

Glanz, J. (2004b). *Teaching 101: Classroom strategies for the beginning teacher.* Thousand Oaks, CA: Corwin.

Glanz, J. (in press). Action research as instructional supervision: Suggestions for principals. *NASSP Bulletin.*

Glanz, J., & Neville, R. F. (1997). *Educational supervision: Perspectives, issues, and controversies.* Norwood, MA: Christopher-Gordon.

Glatthorn, A. A. (2000). *Developing a quality curriculum.* Alexandria, VA: Association for Supervision and Curriculum Development.

Glickman, C. D., Gordon, S. P., & Ross-Gordon, J. M. (1998). *Supervision of instruction: A developmental approach.* Boston: Allyn & Bacon.

Glickman, C. D., Gordon, S. P., & Ross-Gordon, J. M. (2005). *SuperVision and instructional leadership: A developmental approach* (6th ed.). Boston: Allyn & Bacon.

Goldhammer, R. (1969). *Clinical supervision: Special methods for the supervision of teachers.* New York: Holt, Rinehart, & Winston.

Goldhammer, R., Anderson, R. H., & Krajewski, R. J. (1993). *Clinical supervision: Special methods for the supervision of teachers* (3rd ed.). Fort Worth, TX: Harcourt Brace Jovanovich.

Good, T. L., & Brophy, J. E. (1997). *Looking in classrooms* (7th ed.). New York: Addison-Wesley.

Griffin, G. A. (1997). Is staff development supervision? No. In J. Glanz & R. F. Neville (Eds.), *Educational supervision: Perspectives, issues, and controversies* (pp. 162–169). Norwood, MA: Christopher-Gordon.

Hare, W. (1993). *What makes a good teacher: Reflections on some characteristics central to the educational enterprise.* London: Althouse Press.

Jackson, P. W. (1990). *Life in classrooms.* New York: Teachers College Press.

Johnson, D. W., & Johnson, R. T. (1994). *Cooperative learning in the classroom.* Alexandria, VA: Association for Supervision and Curriculum Development.

Johnson, J. (2004). What school leaders want. *Educational Leadership, 61*(7), 24–27.

Lieberman, A. (1995). *The work of restructuring schools: Building from the ground up.* New York: Teachers College Press.

Marzano, R. J., Pickering, D. J., & Pollock, J. E. (2001). *Classroom instruction that works: Research-based strategies for increasing student achievement.* Alexandria, VA: Association for Supervision and Curriculum Development.

Matthew, L. J., & Crow, G. M. (2003). *Being and becoming a principal: Role conceptions for contemporary assistant principals and principals.* Boston: Allyn & Bacon.

Mills, G. E. (2002). *Action research: A guide for the teacher researcher* (2nd ed.). Englewood Cliffs, NJ: Prentice Hall.

Mintrop, H. (2002). Educating student teachers to teach in a constructivist way: Can it all be done? *Teachers College Record, 103*(2). Retrieved February 16, 2005, from http://tcrecord.frameworkers.com/content.asp?contentid=10726

Neill, M. (2003). The dangers of testing. *Educational Leadership, 60*, 43–46.

Nelson, T. (2003). Editor's introduction: In response to increasing state and national control over the teacher education profession. *Teacher Education Quarterly, 30*, 3–8.

Northern Valley Regional High School District. (2000). *Differentiated supervision.* Damerest, NJ: Author.

O'Day, J. A. (2002). Complexity, accountability, and school improvement. *Harvard Educational Review, 72*, 293–329.

Ornstein, A. C. (1990). *Institutionalized learning in America.* New Brunswick, NJ: Transaction.

Osterman, K., & Kottkamp, R. (2004). *Reflective practice for educators: Improving schooling through professional development* (2nd ed.). Thousand Oaks, CA: Corwin.

Pajak, E. (2000). *Approaches to clinical supervision: Alternatives for improving instruction* (2nd ed.). Norwood, MA: Christopher-Gordon.

Portin, B. (with Schneider, P., DeArmond, M., & Gundlach, L.). (2003). *Making sense of leading schools: A study of the school principalship.* Retrieved February 19, 2005, from www.crpe.org/pubs/pdf/Making Sense_PortinWeb.pdf

Portin, B. (2004). The roles that principals play. *Educational Leadership, 61*(7), 14–18.

Reiman, A. J., & Thies-Sprinthall, L. (1998). *Mentoring and supervision for teacher development.* New York: Longman.

Rodgers, C. (2002). Seeing student learning: Teacher change and the role of reflection. *Harvard Educational Review, 72,* 230–253.

Ruebling, C. E., Stow, S. B., Kayona, F. A., & Clarke, N. A. (2004). Instructional leadership: An essential ingredient for improving student learning. *Educational Forum, 68,* 243–253.

Schlechty, P. C. (1990). *Schools for the twenty-first century: Leadership imperatives for cultural reform.* San Francisco: Jossey-Bass.

Schon, D. A. (1987). *Educating the reflective practitioner: Toward a new design for thinking and learning in the professional.* San Francisco: Jossey-Bass.

Schon, D. A. (1988). Coaching reflective teaching. In P. P. Grimmett & G. F. Erickson (Eds.), *Reflection in teacher education* (pp. 19–30). New York: Teachers College Press.

Showers, B., & Joyce, B. (1996). The evolution of peer coaching. *Educational Leadership, 53*(6), 12–16.

Speck, M. (1998). *The principalship: Building a learning community.* Upper Saddle River, NJ: Merrill.

Squires, D. A., Huitt, W. G., & Segars, J. K. (1984). *Effective schools and classrooms: A research-based perspective.* Alexandria, VA: Association for Supervision and Curriculum Development.

Starratt, R. J. (1995). *Leaders with vision: The quest for school renewal.* Thousand Oaks, CA: Corwin.

Stronge, J. H. (2002). *Qualities of effective teachers.* Alexandria, VA: Association for Supervision and Curriculum Development.

Sullivan, S. (1999). Cycles of reflective practice: Building a sense of efficacy in the classroom supervisor. *Educational Leadership and Administration, 11,* 35–45.

Sullivan, S., & Glanz, J. (2000). *Supervision in practice: The video.* Thousand Oaks, CA: Corwin.

Sullivan, S., & Glanz, J. (2005). *Supervision that improves teaching: Strategies and techniques* (2nd ed.). Thousand Oaks, CA: Corwin.

Twomey Fosnet, C. (Ed.). (1996). *Constructivism: Theory, perspectives, and practice.* New York: Teachers College Press.

Tyler, R. W. (1949). *Basic principles of curriculum and instruction.* Chicago: University of Chicago Press.

Vygotski, L. S. (1986). *Thought and language.* Cambridge: MIT Press.

Waters, J. T., Marzano, R. J., & McNulty, B. (2004). Leadership that sparks learning. *Educational Leadership, 61*(7), 48–51.

Weller, R. (1997). *Verbal communication in instructional supervision.* New York: Teachers College Press.

Whitaker, K. S. (1995). Principal burnout: Implications for professional development. *Journal of Personnel Evaluation in Education, 9,* 287–296.

Wiles, J., & Bondi, J. (1998). *Curriculum development: A guide to practice.* Upper Saddle River, NJ: Prentice Hall.

Willerman, M., McNeely, S. L., & Koffman, E. C. (1991). *Teachers helping teachers: Peer observation and assistance.* New York: Praeger.

Wilmore, E. L. (2002). *Principal leadership: Applying the new Educational Leadership Constituent Council (ELCC) standards.* Thousand Oaks, CA: Corwin.

Wilmore, E. L. (2004). *Principal induction: A standards-based model for administrator development.* Thousand Oaks, CA: Corwin.

Young, P. G. (2004). *You have to go to school—You're the principal: 101 tips to make it better for your students, your staff, and yourself.* Thousand Oaks, CA: Corwin.

Zepeda, S. (2003a). *Instructional supervision: Applying tools and concepts.* Larchmont, NY: Eye on Education.

Zepeda, S. (2003b). *The principal as instructional leader: A handbook for supervisors.* Larchmont, NY: Eye on Education.

Index

Note: Page references marked *t* are tables; those marked *f* are figures

**CORWIN
PRESS**

The Corwin Press logo—a raven striding across an open book—represents the union of courage and learning. Corwin Press is committed to improving education for all learners by publishing books and other professional development resources for those serving the field of PreK–12 education. By providing practical, hands-on materials, Corwin Press continues to carry out the promise of its motto: **"Helping Educators Do Their Work Better."**